Sudha Bhuchar and Kristine Landon-Smith

A Fine Balance

based on the novel by Rohinton Mistry

Methuen Drama

Published by Methuen Drama, 2007

1 3 5 7 9 10 8 6 4 2

Methuen Drama
A & C Black Publishers Limited
38 Soho Square
London W1D 3HB
www.acblack.com

Based on the novel by Rohinton Mistry, *A Fine Balance*
(Faber and Faber Limited, 1996)

Copyright © 2007
Sudha Bhuchar and Kristine Landon-Smith

Sudha Bhuchar and Kristine Landon-Smith have asserted
their rights under the Copyright, Designs and Patents Act, 1988,
to be identified as the authors of this work

ISBN: 978 0 713 68823 8

A CIP catalogue record for this book
is available from the British Library

Typeset by Country Setting, Kingsdown, Kent
Printed in the UK by CPI Bookmarque, Croydon, CR0 4TD

tamasha hampstead theatre

Tamasha in association with **hampstead**theatre

a fine balance

adapted by **Sudha Bhuchar** and **Kristine Landon-Smith**
based on the novel by **Rohinton Mistry**

Tamasha and **hampstead**theatre
gratefully acknowledge the support of

Bank of Ireland   LONDON COUNCILS   Camden
Funded by Camden Council   ARTS COUNCIL ENGLAND

This play was first performed at Hampstead Theatre, London on Wednesday 11 January 2006 with the following cast:

Nusswan / Ibrahim / Thakur Dharamsi / Ensemble	Sagar Arya
Dina Dalal / Ensemble	Sudha Bhuchar
Monkey Man / Beggarmaster / Ashraf / Ensemble	Shiv Grewal
Maneck / Shankar / Potency Peddlar / Ensemble	Divian Ladwa
Rajaram / Ensemble	Narinder Samra
Omprakash / Ensemble	Amit Sharma
Ishvar / Ensemble	Rehan Sheikh
Mrs Gupta / Ruby / Ensemble	Sameena Zehra

A Fine Balance

Rajaram / Ashraf / Ensemble	Saikat Ahamed
Ishvar / Ensemble	Sagar Arya
Dina Dalal / Ensemble	Sudha Bhuchar
Mrs Gupta / Ruby / Ensemble	Rina Fatania
Monkey Man / Beggarmaster / Ensemble	Taylan Halici
Nusswan / Ibrahim / Thakur Dharamsi / Ensemble	Tony Jayawardena
Maneck / Shankar / Potency Peddlar / Ensemble	Divian Ladwa
Omprakash / Ensemble	Amit Sharma

Director	Kristine Landon-Smith
Designer	Sue Mayes
Original Score	Felix Cross
Movement	Lawrence Evans
Lighting Design	Natasha Chivers
Sound Design	Mike Furness
Puppetry	Lyndie Wright, Sarah Wright & Ronnie Le Drew
Costume Supervisor	Hilary Lewis

Production Manager	Dennis Charles
Company Stage Manager	Kirsten Turner
Deputy Stage Manager	Charlie Parkin
Assistant Stage Manager	Fern Christie
Assistant Stage Manager / Wardrobe Mistress	Hayley Spicer

Set constructed by	All Scene All Props
Set painted by	James Rowse of Decorative Art Projects
Backdrop painted by	Andy Greenfield
Costumes made by	Judith Clarke, Penny Hadrill, Chloe Stapleton

Tamasha and Hampstead Theatre would like to thank:
Kev Heyes at Theatre Clwyd, British Library, Cobra Beer Ltd, Faber & Faber,
Homepride, www.sillyjokes.co.uk, Westmill Foods

A Fine Balance lasts for approximately 2 hours and 30 minutes including a 20 minute interval

Biographies

Saikat Ahamed
Rajaram / Ashraf / Ensemble

Saikat has just finished working with the BBC Radio Drama Company after being awarded the Norman Beaton Fellowship last year, and plays the regular character of Vinnie in Silver Street on BBC Asian Network. Theatre credits include Sajit Khan in *East is East* (Oldham Coliseum), *Journey to the West* for Tara Arts (national tour), Mercutio in *Romeo and Juliet* at the Lancaster Grand and James in Polka Theatre's production of *James and the Giant Peach*. Screen credits include *Afterlife* (Scary Films / ITV), *7/7 Attack on London* (Mentorn Productions / Channel Five), *It Was An Accident* (Burkett Pictures) and his screen debut, *East is East* (Assassin Films / Channel Four).

Sagar Arya
Ishvar / Ensemble

Sagar's stage career began at three with Brecht's *Caucasian Chalk Circle*. He remains an integral part of the Indian People's Theatre Association and is a senior member of Naseeruddin Shah's theatre group Motley. Sagar played the boy in Beckett's *Waiting for Godot* (1982) going on to play Lucky (1999). He worked with Fritz Bennewitz in Goethe's *Faust* at the National Centre for the Performing Arts. Sagar debuted in London in the West End with *Twelfth Night* (2004). Sagar's television work spans India and the UK. His stint in London began hosting Zee TV's *Heart to Heart*. Sagar presented the Zee Cine Awards 2005 for UK television. He has also appeared in *Doctor Who*, *Life on Mars* and *Casualty*. Recently, his interpretation of Afghan immigrant Kamaal Aziz for BBC Asian Network's *Silver Street* won acclaim. Other radio credits include *Lysistrata*, *Bombay Talkies* and *A Suitable Boy*. His film credits include Merchant Ivory's *In Custody*, *Aastha*, *Fiza* and *Meenaxi*. Upcoming film releases are *Red Mercury*, *Stuart a Life Backwards* and *Jhoom Barabar Jhoom*. Sagar is also an award-winning still photographer, and has worked as assitant cinematographer on *Bride and Prejudice*, *Gaja Gamini* and *Moksh*. He lives in Camden with his writer wife.

Sudha Bhuchar
Adaptor / Dina Dalal / Ensemble

Sudha is joint founder and Artistic Director of Tamasha, and is both an actor and playwright. Her many acting credits include *Murder* (BBC) by Abi Morgan, *EastEnders* (BBC), *Doctors* (BBC), *Holby City* (BBC) and *Haroun and the Sea of Stories* (Royal National Theatre), and she is a regular on the BBC radio drama *Silver Street*. Her writing credits for Tamasha include *Balti Kings, Fourteen Songs, Two Weddings and a Funeral, Strictly Dandia* (in which she also performed) and in May 2006, her first children's play, *Child of the Divide*. She writes regularly with Shaheen Khan and their many credits include three series of *Girlies* for BBC Radio 4 and *Balti Kings* (the stage play, as well as a six part series for Radio 4). Their screenplay, *The House across the Street*, has been shown on BBC4 as part of a new writers' initiative, and they have co-written an episode of Doctors for the BBC. Sudha also co-wrote a short film *Midnight Feast*, which was screened at the 11th Raindance Film Festival and most recently at the Tongues on Fire festival in London. Sudha jointly won, with Kristine Landon-Smith, the 2005 Asian Women of Achievement Award for Arts and Culture.

Natasha Chivers
Lighting Designer

Designs include: *Sunday in the Park with George* (Wyndhams Theatre), winner of an Olivier for Best Lighting Design; *Encore George Piper Dances* (Sadlers Wells / tour); *Kindertransport* (Shared Experience / national tour); *Wolves in the Walls* (Improbable / National Theatre Of Scotland); *Pool (No Water), Hymns, Peepshow* and *Tiny Dynamite* (Frantic Assembly / Lyric Hammersmith – national and international tours); *HOME Glasgow* and *Mary Stuart* (National Theatre Scotland); *Jerusalem* and *Playhouse Creatures* (West Yorkshire Playhouse); *Palace Dreams* and *Renaissance* (Greenwich and Docklands International Festival); *Dirty Wonderland* (Frantic Assembly / Brighton Festival); *A Fine Balance* (Tamasha / Hampstead Theatre); *Mercury Fur* (Plymouth Drum); *Small Things* and *Pyrenees* (Tron Theatre Glasgow); *The*

Bomb-itty of Errors (The Ambassadors Theatre); *The Straits* (59 East 59, New York / Hampstead Theatre); Liverpool Everyman 40th Anniversary Season including *Urban Legend* and *The Kindness Of Strangers*; and *The Entertainer* and *Who's Afraid Of Virginia Woolfe* (Liverpool Playhouse). Future projects include: *Moments* (Legs on the Wall, Sydney, Australia - International Fellowship Award Summer 2007); work with the *Ballet Boyz* at Sadlers Wells; and RFH opening gala.

Felix Cross
Original Score
Felix Cross is a composer, playwright and director and has been the Artistic Director of NITRO / Black Theatre Co-op since 1996. His work includes *Passports to the Promised Land* (NITRO), *Blues For Railton* (Albany Empire), *Glory!* (Temba / Derby Playhouse), *Mass Carib* (Albany Empire / South Bank / National tour). Music and lyrics include *Jekyll & Hyde* and *The Bottle Imp* (both books by Graham Devlin, Major Road), *The Evocation of Papa Mas'* (Told by an Idiot / NITRO), *Tricksters' Payback* (Black Theatre Co-op), *Pinchy Kobi and the Seven Duppies* (The Posse, Tricycle Theatre / Stratford East). Play scripts include *The Wedding Dance* (NITRO), *Slamdunk* (NITRO) and *Up Against the Wall* (co-written with Paulette Randall, Black Theatre Co-op). He composed *Integration Octet* (for string quartet and steel pan quartet − Aldeburgh / Royal Festival Hall) and he has also composed for at least seventy productions in theatre, radio, TV and film, including *Macbeth* (national and world tours) and *Talking to Terrorists* (both for Out of Joint) and *Ryman and the Sheikh* and *Ghostdancing* for Tamasha. He has directed *The Panbeaters* (Greenwich Theatre), plays for Radio 4, as well as several productions for NITRO including *The Wedding Dance* (co-directed with Debra Michaels), *Mass Carib* in Trafalgar Square, *Slamdunk* (co-directed with Benji Reid) and *ICED*.

Lawrence Evans
Movement Director
Lawrence works as a director, movement director and actor. He was nominated for an Olivier Award for his work with Tony Harrison at the National Theatre. He has worked with the poet and playwright on all his site-specific theatre pieces touring to Greece, Austria, Sweden and Bradford. He received a Best Actor Award from the Liverpool Echo and Daily Post Northwest Arts Awards and his co-written play *Lives Worth Living* is published by Heinemann. His work as an actor includes small, middle and large scale touring nationally and internationally, many of the regional Repertory Theatres throughout the UK as well as the National Theatre, NT studio, Cheek by Jowl, the Young Vic and Northern Broadsides. As a Movement Director he has done over 40 productions. As a Director his work includes the Oxfordshire Touring Theatre Company [OTTC], *Stravinsky's Soldiers Tale* with Anthony Marwood for the Academy of St. Martin in the Fields, the New York Showcase for the Conference of Drama Schools and for Theatre Centre as Associate Director in 2001/2. In Drama Schools he has directed at Rose Bruford, Italia Conti, East 15, ALRA and Drama Centre. Other directing includes Theatre Centre, Polka and London Bubble. This is Lawrence's fifth production for Tamasha.

Rina Fatania
Mrs Gupta / Ruby / Ensemble
Rina trained for three years at the Central School of Speech and Drama. Her recent credits include *Child of the Divide* (Tamasha), Agnes in *Meri Christmas* (Rifco Arts), Kiran in *The Deranged Marriage* (Rifco Arts), *Pushpa / Hina Shah* in Strictly Dandia (Tamasha), Swing cover for Shanti and Mumtaaz in *Bombay Dreams* (Really Useful Group), Marijana / Dunzazaad in *Arabian Nights* (MAC), Zara Khan in *Dil Ke Baat* (Women in Theatre), Euphranor / Bully in *Before The City* (Vital Stages) and Dame Dolly in *Puff the Magic Dragon* for Hurricane Productions. Other roles include Billy Downs in *The Libertine*, Rhonda in *The Secret Rapture*, Juliette in *Mephisto*, Jacqueline / Irene in *Reader*, Rachel in *The Sea*, Grusha in *The Caucasian Chalk Circle*, Mistress Overdone / Mariana in *Measure for Measure*, Moth in *Love's Labour's Lost* and Kaleria in *Summerfolk*. On radio she has played Meghna in *Oceans Unite Us* and Boetian / Ensemble in *Lysistrata* for the BBC World Service.

Mike Furness
Sound Designer

Theatre sound designs include: *All's Well That Ends Well* and *As You Like It* (RSC), *Blues In The Night, The Witches, Ladyday, The BFG* (West End), *Mother Courage* (National Theatre). He has also designed sound for: Birmingham Rep, Manchester Library, The Kings Head, The Tricycle, Paines Plough, Theatre Royal Stratford East and the Brighton and Edinburgh Festivals. Recent sound designs include *Babe* (Regents Park Open Air Theatre 2006), *On Religion* (Soho Theatre), *Someone Else's Shoes* (Soho Theatre). He has produced a series of audio dramas for The Natural History Museum and also a number of Talking Books. His production of music for fireworks ranges from events such as The Royal Windsor Horse Show to the launch of the P&O Cruise Ship "Oriana". The majority of his work is designing sound systems for concerts, corporate, and other live events worldwide, most recently for Ford, EMI & MTV. This is his seventh sound design for Tamasha, including *The Trouble with Asian Men* and *Child of the Divide*.

Taylan Halici
Monkey Man / Beggarmaster / Ensemble

Recent theatre credits include: *Birds without Wings* (Eastern Angles), *Babel Junction* (Hackney Empire Bullion), *Hoxton Story* (The Red Room), *Close To Home* (Theatre Alibi), *The Pink Bits* (Riverside Studios), *Night Just Before the Forests, Rosencrantz & Guildenstern Are Dead, Marat-Sade* (Arcola), *Agamemnon* (Foursight TC). As a member of Mkultra Performance Collective, Taylan has performed in site specific, studio based and durational performances in London and for The Turin International Theatre Festival, including: *Once Seen, 30000 Lies or More, 5X5, Always, Left-Long*. Solo performances include: *Go Home* (2004: Arcola, Chelsea Theatre, Bristol Old Vic Mayfest), *Slim Pickens* (2006: Hackney Empire Bullion).

Tony Jayawardena
Nusswan / Ibrahim / Thakur
Dharamsi / Ensemble

Tony graduated from the Guildhall School of Music and Drama in 2003. He was awarded the Gold Medal for his theatrical performances at drama school and graduated with honours.

Drama school productions include: *Pravda* (Andrew May), *Singer* (Pete Singer), *The Old School Bachelor* (Sir Joseph Wittoll), *Trojan Women* (Agamemnon), *Landscape* (Duff), *The King of Hearts* (Genevieve), *A Midsummer Night's Dream* (Demetrius, Snout and Mustardseed), *Barbarians* (Redozubov and Roberto Zucco). Since leaving drama school Tony has been busy working in film, television and theatre. His film credits include *Chasing Liberty* for Warner Brothers. Television credits include: *Holby City* (BBC) where he played Charlie Swanton; *Doctors* (BBC) as Dev Desai; *Blair* (Mentorn) as Security Guard; *Chucklevision* (BBC) as Mr Florence and *Hotel Babylon* (Carnival Films). Tony made his theatrical debut in *Othello* and *The Sneeze* for Good Company Shakespeare Productions Ltd and played Baloo in the UK tour of *The Jungle Book* for Birmingham Stage Company. He appeared in Tamasha's *Child of the Divide* (Polka Theatre / WebPlay UK & US tour), a reading of *Wanted for Marriage* and a production of *Behna* (Soho Theatre). Last Christmas, Tony appeared at The Broadway, Barking playing the Genie in *Aladdin*.

Divian Ladwa
Maneck / Shankar / Peddler / Ensemble

Divian has appeared in Tamasha's last three productions: *Child of the Divide* (Polka Theatre / WebPlay UK & US tour), *A Fine Balance* (Hampstead Theatre) and *The Trouble with Asian Men* (artsdepot / Soho Theatre and tour). His other theatre credits include performing at The Edinburgh International Festival (The King's Theatre) and touring nationally with Tamasha's *Strictly Dandia* (including Lyric Hammersmith). He has appeared in Fluxx Improvisational Theatre Company's *Human Vs Animal, Alls Hallow* and *Even with Trudie and Jeff* and various shows of *The Visitor* and a London tour of Spare Tyre's *Burning*. He was also a sword fighter at last year's Roman Season at The Globe, featuring in their Gladiatorial Exhibitions as a Parthinian Secutor. TV and film credits include Channel 4's *School's Out*, short features by Imagination Films including *Modern Chivalry* and *Painful Love, Wing Kit Loois' Tomorrow* where he co-choreographed the movie's fight scene, and Minamon Film's *Governor's Hearing* as Anil Patel. Divian can be seen playing Rahim Begum in the British feature film *Saxon* (dir. Greg Loftin) and he has just finished post-production on his own short film *The Boxer*, adapted from a play he is writing.

Kristine Landon-Smith
Adaptor / Director

Kristine is joint founder and Artistic Director of Tamasha and has directed all of the company's shows. Her 1996 production, *East is East*, was nominated for an Olivier award and her original production of *Fourteen Songs, Two Weddings and a Funeral* won the Barclays Theatre Award for Best New Musical. Her production of *Strictly Dandia*, was a sell-out success at the Lyric Hammersmith in both 2004 and 2005. Kristine's freelance credits include directing with the Royal Court Theatre, Bristol Old Vic, Palace Theatre Westcliff, Nitro, Yellow Earth Theatre and more recently with the Royal Danish Theatre, where she directed the *Con:FUSIONS* workshop in Autumn 2005, aimed at developing cultural diversity in Scandinavian theatre. Her first short film Midnight Feast was screened at the 11th Raindance Film Festival and, most recently, the Tongues on Fire festival in London. Kristine's radio credits for BBC include *A Yearning, Women of the Dust*, which won CRE Race in the Media Awards, and an adaptation of *Lysistrata* by Ranjit Bolt for the BBC World Service. Most recently, Kristine directed *The Trouble with Asian Men* (artsdepot / Soho Theatre and tour) and Tamasha's first children's play *Child of the Divide* (Polka Theatre / WebPlay UK & US tour). Kristine jointly won, with Sudha Bhuchar, the 2005 Asian Women of Achievement Award for Arts and Culture.

Sue Mayes
Designer

Trained at Central School of Art and Design (Central St. Martins) in the 1970s. Her career started at Ipswich Rep, from where she went on to residencies at the Belgrade Theatre in Education Coventry, Contact Theatre Manchester and The Everyman Theatre Liverpool. Her freelance work has included designs for The Royal Shakespeare Company; Talawa Theatre Company; Bristol Old Vic Theatre; and the Theatre Royal Stratford East. Recent designs include *Turn of the Screw* at the Wolsey Theatre Ipswich and *Kafka's Dick* at Derby Playhouse. Sue teaches regularly at drama schools across London including R.A.D.A

and Guildhall School of Music and Drama, and she has recently moved into film as production designer on *Midnight Feast*, a short film for Tamasha, and *Two Minutes* for the BBC. Sue has designed all of Tamasha's previous productions.

Amit Sharma
Omprakash / Ensemble

Amit is a graduate of Graeae's The Missing Piece 1 project. Amit has appeared in three productions with Tamasha, including the original run of *A Fine Balance* (Hampstead Theatre), *Child of the Divide* (Polka Theatre / WebPlay UK & US tour) and *The Trouble with Asian Men* (artsdepot, Soho Theatre and tour). Other theatre credits include: *Other People's Shoes* (Theatre Royal Stratford East and Spare Tyre), *Woyzeck, Into the Mystic, The Trouble with Richard, Diary of an Action Man* (Graeae), *Granny and the Gorilla* (Unicorn), *Reality Check* (Theatre Centre) and *Something Else* (Tall Stories). He was also Assistant Director on *The Changeling* (Graeae) and *The Dysasters Of John Daniell* (Immediate Theatre). TV and film credits include: *Tikkabilla* (BBC), *The Robinsons* (BBC), *Waiting for Movement* (Red Leader). Amit co-wrote *Stoppage Time* (BBC Radio 4) as well as writing *Indi-yaar* for Paines Plough's Wild Lunch series. If Amit's not doing any of the above then he plays a supporting role to the current FA Cup winners Liverpool Football Club.

Lyndie Wright
Puppetry

Born in South Africa, Lyndie originally came to London to study painting at the Central School of Art. After initially working as a painter, in 1961 she founded The Little Angel Theatre with her husband John Wright. She transformed a derelict temperance hall in Islington into a magical theatre designed especially for children and for the presentation of marionette shows. She continued to work there for the next forty-two years, designing most of the company's innovative and highly acclaimed shows while working as both operator and maker. In 2002, Lyndie retired from The Little Angel although she has continued to work with them, as well as numerous others, including the RSC, the National Theatre, the Munich Puppet Players and the Brandenburg Theatre (Germany).

Rohinton Mistry

Rohinton Mistry is the author of a collection of short
stories, *Tales from Firozsha Baag* (1987), and three
internationally acclaimed novels that have all been
shortlisted for the Booker Prize.

His first novel, *Such a Long Journey*, published
in 1991 won the Governor General's Award, The
Commonwealth Writers Prize for Best Book and the
WH Smith / Books in Canada First Novel Award. It was
made into an acclaimed feature film in 1998.

A Fine Balance, published in 1995, was awarded the
Giller Prize, the Commonwealth Writers Prize, the
Royal Society of Literature's Winifred Holtby Award
and Denmark's ALOA Prize.

His most recent novel is *Family Matters*, published in
2002. It won the Kiriyama Pacific Rim Book Prize and
was a finalist for the IMPAC Dublin Literary Award.

Born in Bombay, Rohinton Mistry has lived in Canada
since 1975. His work has been published in over
twenty-five languages.

tamasha

About Tamasha

Tamasha is an award-winning theatre company led by director Kristine Landon-Smith and actor / playwright Sudha Bhuchar.

From adaptations of classic literature, through improvised comedy and vibrant musicals, to groundbreaking new writing, Tamasha has played a key role in driving the crossover of Asian culture into the British mainstream. Successes like *East is East, Fourteen Songs, Two Weddings and a Funeral, Strictly Dandia* and *The Trouble with Asian Men* have won acclaim from critics and audiences alike, and have launched the careers of a number of well-known British Asian artists.

Since its founding in 1989, Tamasha has produced sixteen new plays. Its work has won a TMA Barclays Theatre Award for Best Musical, a Writers Guild award, two CRE Race in the Media awards and a BBC Asia award for Achievement in the Arts, as well as receiving an Olivier nomination for Best New Comedy. In 2005, Kristine and Sudha were jointly awarded the Asian Women of Achievement award in the Arts and Culture category.

Alongside its touring productions, the Company nurtures emerging talent through Tamasha Developing Artists, an ongoing programme of professional development initiatives for writers, directors, designers and performers.

For more about Tamasha's work, or to join the mailing list, visit www.tamasha.org.uk

Tamasha Theatre Company
Unit 220 Great Guildford Business Square
30 Great Guildford Street
London SE1 0HS

t. 020 7633 2270
f. 020 7021 0421
e. info@tamasha.org.uk
w. www.tamasha.org.uk

Support Tamasha

As a charity, Tamasha needs to raise an additional £100,000 every year from private sources to sustain its pioneering programme of work and to enable its ongoing development. A large part of Tamasha's work - from productions and touring to the training of talented young artists - is dependent on the generosity of its supporters.

If you would like to help Tamasha, there are numerous ways in which you can get involved: you can join our Friends Scheme from £60 a year; make a donation to the Tamasha Fund from £250; or support us as a business by becoming a Corporate Sponsor.

Your donation could help fund a new writing commission, a bursary for a talented artist, the costs of a rehearsal room or one of our productions. Donations of all sizes are welcome and every penny goes directly towards projects, ensuring that Tamasha continues to flourish.

If you are interested in knowing more please contact Rebecca Russell on 020 7633 2277 or email rebecca@tamasha.org.uk.

We are very grateful to the following for their support of our work:

Individual Supporters

Anuj J Chande; Régis Cochefert; Shernaz Engineer; Samar Hamid; Zahid Kasim; Zulf Masters OBE; Nina & Nilesh Majeethia; Deepa Patel; Kiran Patel; James L. Prouty; Felix Rigg; Mayank & Vandana Shah; Rahul & Rita Sharma; Ramesh & Ella Vala; together with those who wish to remain anonymous.

Trusts & Foundations

Coutts Charitable Trust; D'Oyly Carte Charitable Trust; Esmée Fairbairn Foundation; Garfield Weston Foundation; The John S Cohen Foundation; The Peggy Ramsay Foundation; The Stanley Picker Trust; Unity Theatre Trust.

Corporate Sponsors

Bank of Ireland; Cobra Beer Ltd; Erinaceous Auctions

About **hampstead**theatre

hampsteadtheatre is one of the UK's leading new writing venues housed in a magnificent purpose-built state-of-the-art theatre – a company that is fast approaching its fiftieth year of operation.

hampsteadtheatre has a mission: to find, develop, and produce new plays to the highest possible standards, for as many people as we can encourage to see them. Its work is both national and international in its scope and ambition.

hampsteadtheatre exists to take risks and to discover the talent of the future. New writing is our passion. We consistently create the best conditions for writers to flourish and are rewarded with diverse award-winning and far-reaching plays.

The list of playwrights who had their early work produced at **hampstead**theatre who are now filling theatres all over the country and beyond include Mike Leigh, Michael Frayn, Brian Friel, Terry Johnson, Hanif Kureishi, Simon Block, Abi Morgan, Rona Munro, Tamsin Oglesby, Harold Pinter, Philip Ridley, Shelagh Stephenson, Debbie Tucker Green, Crispin Whittell and Roy Williams. The careers of actors Jude Law, Alison Steadman, Jane Horrocks and Rufus Sewell were launched at **hampstead**theatre.

Each year the theatre invites the most exciting writers around to write for us. At least half of these playwrights will be emerging writers who are just hitting their stride - writers who we believe are on the brink of establishing themselves as important new voices. We also ask mid-career and mature playwrights to write for us on topics they are burning to explore.

The success of **hampstead**theatre is yours to support

Since opening our stunning award-winning building, we have presented sixteen world premieres, three European premieres and fourteen London premieres. We have commissioned thirty-two writers, transferred two plays to the West End, and six of our playwrights have won prestigious Most Promising Playwright awards. We also have one of the most extensive education and participation programmes of all theatres in London.

Our artistic achievements have inspired increasing critical and commercial success. This has been made possible by the many individuals, trusts and companies that have already chosen to invest in our creativity. To secure our bright future we need your support.

If you would like more information about supporting **hampstead**theatre and helping us to nurture the new talents and audiences of the future, please email development@hampsteadtheatre.com or call Tamzin Robertson on 020 7449 4171.

hampsteadtheatre would like to thank the following for their support:
Abbey Charitable Trust; Acacia Charitable Trust; Anglo American; Arts & Business; Awards for All; The Alchemy Foundation; Auerbach Trust Charity; BBC Children in Need; Bennetts Associates; Big Lottery Fund; Blick Rothenberg; Bridge House Estates Trust Fund; Community Chest; Community Fund; The John S Cohen Foundation; D'Oyly Carte Charitable Trust; The Dorset Foundation; The Eranda Foundation; The Ernest Cook Trust; European Association of Jewish Culture; Garrick Charitable Trust; Gerald Ronson Foundation; GHP Group; Goldschmidt and Howland; The Goldsmiths Company; The Hampstead & Highgate Express; Help a London Child; Harold Hyam Wingate Foundation; The Jack Petchey Foundation; Jacobs Charitable Trust; John Lyon's Charitable Trust; Lloyds TSB Foundation for England and Wales; Kennedy Leigh Charitable Trust; Local Network Fund; Markson Pianos; Milly Apthorp Charitable Trust; The Mirianog Trust; The Morel Trust: The Nöel Coward Foundation; Notes Productions Ltd; Ocado; The Ormonde & Mildred Duveen Trust; Parkheath Estates: The Paul Hamlyn Foundation: The Rayne Foundation; Reed Elsevier; Richard Grand Foundation; Richard Reeves Foundation; Royal Victoria Hall Foundation; Samuel French; The Shoresh Foundation; Sir John Cass' Foundation; Solomon Taylor Shaw: Sweet and Maxwell; Towry Law; The Vintners' Company; World Jewish Relief; Charles Wolfson Foundation.

hampsteadtheatre would also like to thank the numerous individuals who have supported the theatre through our Luminary scheme.

Verity

recruitment you can trust●

Verity Recruitment Group

For Supply Teachers
(Primary & Secondary)
Throughout Greater London

Telephone: 020 7629 8786
www.verityeducation.com

For Secretarial and Ancillary Staff
Throughout London and South East

Telephone: 020 7493 0437
www.verityappointments.com

INVESTOR IN PEOPLE

Recruitment &
Employment
Confederation

A Fine Balance

Characters
in order of appearance

Shankar, *a young beggar*
Dina, *Parsi widow, early forties*
Om, *young low-caste tailor*
Ishvar, *middle-aged low-caste tailor, Om's uncle*
Maneck, *seventeen-year-old student*
Woman, *in slum*
Rajaram, *a hair-collector*
Monkeyman, *itinerant performer*
Vishram, *tea-stall owner*
Mrs Gupta, *owner of a clothing export company*
Ibrahim, *rent-collector*
Nusswan, *Dina's older brother*
Beggarmaster
Ashraf, *tailor and friend to Om and Ishvar*
Potency Peddlar
Thakur Dharamsi, *landowner*
Ruby, *Nusswan's wife*

Tailors, workers on the building site, market vendors, etc.

Location

A dusty, open, fluid space which serves as multiple locations.
A backdrop with a portrait of Mrs Gandhi hangs behind.

Act One

Prologue

Shankar, *a beggar, crawls on his gaddi and talks directly to the audience.*

Shankar (*calling*)   Are babu ek paisa de do. Spare a paisa for a poor beggar. Look at me – Shankar, but everybody calls me Worm . . . Before I got this gaddi I used to crawl around. No legs, can't walk . . . Just one paisa . . .

He doesn't get any money.

Bhenchod! Suited and booted, the world at your feet . . . Don't you know a beggar's blessing is better than a eunuch's curse?

Seeing a pretty woman:

Arey behna, with your pretty face I bet your man keeps you in style. Who will caress my rough cheek and hold me in their warm embrace? . . . Spare a paisa for the less fortunate!

To another man:

Eh, babu. Ek paisa, just one paisa . . . for dry roti and daal . . . Stomach is empty . . . Give in your children's name . . . The country is in Emergency . . . Evil eye is everywhere . . . Your charity will keep your innocents safe . . . You look at me, you turn your face, you walk past. But from my pavement throne, I see everything.

He picks out a couple of members of the audience.

I can see there is something deep troubling you – and you, the lady beside you, she is not happy with you. Laughter, pain, happiness and sorrow. Nothing goes past me. Everyone comes to this city by the sea to try their luck but only the lines on your palm decide your fate! . . . You believe or you don't.

Dina Dalal *walks past* **Shankar**. *He calls out to her:*

Shankar   Babu ek paisa de do. Sorry, memsahib, take pity
on a poor beggar. Your home will flourish! Your children will
blossom!

Dina *chucks him a paisa in his tin. She is clearly lost.*

Shankar   Madam, you look lost. This part of the city is not
for ladies like you. I'm like *A to Z*, where you want to go?

Dina   Tailors' alley.

Shankar   You looking for tailors? I know just the people.
Trust me . . . Round the corner, to the right. Ask for Om and
Ishvar Darzi. They trained. Good experience.

Dina *goes.*

Shankar   My friends Om and Ishvar, they will be pleased
I gave their recommendation. They're new to this city. They
don't know its ways. How about that? Me a poor beggar. I
might have changed their fate. Between you and me, they had
to leave their village, go AWOL . . . keep a low profile . . . you
understand? This city is like a good mistress . . . she'll keep
your secrets. You can forget your past and look to the future . . .

He goes off with his cry for money: 'Eh babu ek paisa de do.'

Scene One

Streets of an urban metropolis in India.

Tailors working somewhere in the underbelly of the city.

Tailor 1   Are we going to get any tea today?

Tailor 2   Eh chotu! Chai leke aa. Pani kum.

Om (*about the clothes they're sewing*)   Who needs so many shirts?

Tailor 1   We are earning. What's it to you?

Om   Only for three days. Then what?

Ishvar   God will provide.

Tailor 3   Arey, in this Emergency there is no god.

Tailor 1   Only the goddess.

Ishvar   Who?

Tailor 3   The Iron Widow, smiling from all the posters.

Tailor 2   Worship her and maybe she will bless you.

After a pause **Om** *starts singing.*

Om   'Kya hua jo dil tuta . . . '

Tailor 1   Arey, Hero! Who has broken your heart?

Tailor 2   The girl at the water pipe every morning.

Om   Why you jealous?

Ishvar   Stop dreaming. I will find the girl for you.

Om   Find one for yourself first.

Tailor 1   Is he making tea or cooking nehari?

Dina Dalal *comes looking for tailors.*

Dina   Namaste.

They all greet her.

I'm Dina Dalal. I'm looking for two tailors to work exclusively for me. Permanent job. Koi interested, hai?

Tailor 1   Han han . . . (*Showing his work.*) Dekho.

Dina   Nahin, nahin, finishing is not good.

Tailor 2   Look. Tip-top.

Dina   I want export quality.

Tailor 2   Export quality? This is expert quality.

Dina   Detail has to be good. No crooked collars, uneven hems, mismatched sleeves.

Tailor 2   Han. Han.

Dina   Hours are eight to six. At my house.

Tailor 2   Yeh to nahin ho sakta. Deliver work to us, then no problem.

Dina   Sewing has to be done under my strict supervision, otherwise I lose the contract.

Ishvar   We come to house. Me and my nephew. Ishvar and Om Prakash Darzi. Fully trained. We are apprentice for many years.

Dina   You have experience in ladies' clothes?

Ishvar   Plenty. We can make any fashion you like. Puff sleeves . . . bell bottoms.

Dina   In this job sewing is from paper patterns. Same style, two-dozen, three-dozen.

Ishvar   Repeat pattern is easy for us. You won't be disappointed.

Dina   Eight o'clock every day.

Ishvar   Eight o'clock, nine o'clock, anytime. We are there. Double-stitch, first-class.

Dina *looks at his work.*

Dina   Mm, fine stitching.

She gives him a piece of paper with her address on it.

Here is my address. You come tomorrow morning. We'll give it a try.

Scene Two

Dina's *flat.*

Ishvar *and* **Om** *come on, bringing their machines with them.*

Ishvar   On hire purchase. In three years when payments are complete, they will belong to us.

Dina   And the money I paid just now for your taxi?

Ishvar   Please deduct from our wages.

Dina   Work is from eight to six, with one hour prompt for lunch.

Ishvar   One meal at night is sufficient.

Om   Speak for yourself.

The tailors set up and start to sew.

Dina   These thirty-six dresses are a test. Neatness, accuracy and consistency. I will supervise. My eyes might fail me in threading a needle, but don't think they will miss a crooked seam. Only if Mrs Gupta is satisfied will I get bigger orders.

Om   Who is this Mrs Gupta.?

Dina   Never you mind.

Ishvar   Dinabai, what is this Emergency we hear about?

Dina   Government problems. Games played by people in power. Doesn't affect ordinary people like us.

Om   That's what I said. My uncle likes to worry.

Dina   Oh, and if the rent collector, Ibrahim, sees you coming or going, tell him you are here to do the cooking and cleaning.

Om   You want us to lie?

Ishvar   Han han. Dinabai. Whatever you say.

Maneck *comes running in, wet from his bath.*

Maneck   Dina Auntie, there are worms crawling out of the plughole!

Dina   Just throw some water on them. They will go away.

The tailors clock **Maneck**.

Dina   Maneck is my boarder. He needs peace and quiet to study.

Ishvar   Han. Han.

Dina   Or should I be calling you Mac?

Maneck   I hate that name.

Om   What are you studying?

Maneck   Air conditioning.

Ishvar   What?

Om   That machine that makes the air cold.

Ishvar   And how is your college?

Maneck   Hopeless. But I have to finish it somehow to please my father. Then home I go on the first train.

Ishvar   Soon as we collect some money. We're also going back to find a wife for my nephew.

Om   How many times do I have to say, I'm not getting married?

Ishvar   Look at that sour-lime face.

Dina   Well, the more you sew, the more you earn.

Tailors start sewing again.

Dina (*to* **Maneck**)   Now, have you finished your bath, or the worms have frightened you off?

Maneck   They're disgusting. So many of them.

Dina   Since it's your first day, I'll treat them with phenol but it's very expensive. From tomorrow you'll have to make friends with the worms.

Maneck   Thank you, Auntie.

Dina   Wouldn't want your mum to think I'm not looking after you.

Maneck   No, no . . .

Dina   She's given me strict instructions. Fried eggs floating in butter for your breakfast . . .

Maneck   Anything is better than the college canteen.

Dina   I hope you'll be comfortable here.

Maneck   Of course. You've given me your room . . .

Dina   Just as I'd learned to be alone, I have company.

Maneck *exits*

*The tailors and **Dina** resume sewing. In a dreamlike sequence there is the sound of rain, and **Dina** is pulled towards the verandah window. She looks out and imagines her husband tipping his hat to her. He opens his umbrella and exits. **Dina** stands transfixed at the window. The tailors exit.*

Scene Three

*Slum site, temporary home of **Om** and **Ishvar**.*

Rajaram *enters with his plate of food and starts eating. A **Woman** is there, sifting through her basket of fruit.*

Rajaram   Got something sweet? Banana?

Woman   Bananas I'm saving for Monkeyman. I've got a mango. Too bruised for people with money.

*She cleans it with her spit and gives it to **Rajaram**.*

Rajaram   Clean it with water.

Woman   Where is there water round here?

Om *and* **Ishvar** *arrive and greet* **Rajaram**.

Rajaram   Come sit with me, share my meal.

Ishvar   No, such a long journey from Dinabai's, so we ate at the station.

Rajaram   No, you're new here. It's my duty to look after you.

He goes off to get the food.

Ishvar   So what colour plates and glasses shall we buy?

Om   Doesn't matter.

Ishvar   Towel? The one with yellow flowers?

Om   Doesn't matter.

Ishvar   It'll give a homely feel to this place.

Om   It's a slum.

Woman *gives the tailor a piece of fruit.*

Woman   Eat. Good for your health.

Rajaram *comes back with food for them.* **Ishvar** *puts some of his food onto* **Om**'s *plate.*

Ishvar   In this city, Rajaram, you are looking after strangers. You don't find that in a city.

Rajaram   The city grabs you, sinks its claws into you and refuses to let you go.

Om   Not us, we are here to make some money and hurry back.

Rajaram   That's what we all say.

Om   We have some unfinished business in the village.

Rajaram   Kyon? What have you done?

Ishvar   It is not us who have done. We have been done upon.

Rajaram   To kese chalta he?

Ishvar   Dinabai makes us work hard. There is a long order for dresses.

Rajaram   Good if order is long.

Om   Morning to night we are doing skilled work and still she wants us to pretend we're her maderchod servants who sweep and mop.

Ishvar   It's just a story to prevent trouble with the landlord.

Om   Trouble for whom? For her? Why should I care? If we are dead tomorrow, she'll get two new tailors and we couldn't even afford the ghee and wood for our funeral pyre.

Ishvar   You are forever speaking without thinking. If she gets kicked out of the flat, we have no place to work. Socha he? This is our first decent job since we came to the city.

Om   And I should rejoice for that? Secret destinations where she delivers the dresses. We should work direct for this Mrs Gupta. Cut out Dinabai. She is making money from our sweat without a single stitch from her fingers.

Rajaram   How's her hair?

Ishvar   Her hair?

Rajaram   Baal. Is it long or short?

Om (*indicating with his hand*)   Long down to here, but she keeps it tight like her fist . . . and black. Not one grey hair on her head.

Woman   Be careful talking to him or you'll be bald.

Ishvar   You are a hair-doctor, I think.

Rajaram   Barber. But I gave it up. Got fed up with complaining customers. Too short, too long, puff not big enough, sideburns not wide enough. Every ugly fellow wants to look like a film actor . . . Now I'm a hair-collector.

Ishvar   What do you have to do as a hair-collector?

Rajaram   Collect hair.

Om   And is there money in that?

Rajaram   Very big business. There is great demand for hair in foreign countries.

Ishvar   What do they do with it?

Rajaram   Mostly they wear it. Foreign women enjoy wearing other people's hair. Men also, especially if they are bald. In foreign countries they fear baldness.

Om   And how do you collect the hair? Steal it from people's heads?

Rajaram   I go to pavement barbers. They let me take it in exchange for a packet of blades, or soap, or a comb. In haircutting salons they give it free if I sweep the floor. I'll show you my stock.

He shows them his sacks in the lamp light.

See, short hair. Not more than two, three inches long. Sold by the kilo to the export agent. But look inside this bag. From a ladies' barber. Beautiful . . . no? This is the valuable stuff.

Om (*feeling the hair in the sack*) Feels good. Soft and smooth.

Rajaram   You know, when I find hair like this I always want to meet the woman. I lie awake wondering about her. What does she look like? Why was it cut? For fashion? For punishment? Or did her husband die?

Om   This must have been a rich woman's hair.

Rajaram   And why do you think so?

Om   Because of the fragrance. A poor woman would use raw coconut oil.

Rajaram   Perfectly correct. You have the makings of a hair-collector. Let me know if you get tired of tailoring.

Om   But would I be able to stroke the hair while it's still attached to the woman? All the hair? From top to bottom, and between the legs?

Rajaram   He's a clever rascal, isn't he?

Monkeyman *arrives with a monkey and dog.* **Om** *and* **Ishvar** *react to the dog.* **Woman** *calls over Leila, the monkey.*

Woman   Arey Leila. Idhar aa. Look what I got for you. Pahle chachi ko salaam kar.

Leila makes salaam and holds out her hand.

Monkeyman   Look at her. Holding her hand out for money.

Woman   Here. Take, I kept banana for her.

Monkeyman   Tikka idhar aa.

He takes food out of the monkey's mouth.

What you got in mouth? Left your brother to scavenge in the kachra. You should have seen her today. Playing the shy bride, haina Leila?

Woman (*singing*)   'Raja ki aayegi baraat . . . ' One day we find groom for you.

The dog sniffs around her. She shoos him away.

Monkeyman   Hey, Tikka . . . tomorrow your papa is invited by the Prime Minister . . . Big Congress Party rally. Buses coming to take me. She want to hear things from my lips.

Rajaram   You and thousands of other idiots.

Woman   Tell her to come and see what prosperity we are living in. You also going to this rally?

Rajaram   I'm not giving up a day of hair-collecting to listen to bogus talk and be Mother India's adoring public. You?

Woman   They're paying five rupees and free snack and tea

Om   Let's go.

Ishvar   We have a job. Let the unemployed take tea with the Prime Minister.

Monkeyman   So, Tikka, I am trusting you with your sister.

Woman   Take her with you.

Monkeyman   It's meeting, not circus. They don't want monkey, even though I tell them Leila is like my obedient child. Anyway, she cause trouble . . . Come now. So ja . . . come . . . (*To the monkey.*) Leave banana for breakfast.

Scene Four

Vishram's *restaurant − a roadside stall in the city.*

Vishram *comes on selling his wares.* **Om** *comes on. He notices the poster of Indira Gandhi.*

Om   You too have become a devotee of the goddess?

Vishram   Compulsory prayers. Her presence is protection.

Om   Kya mutlub?

Vishram   I put up her picture and advertise her twenty-point programme and my windows don't get smashed by gorrement vandals.

Om   Twenty points?

Vishram   She wants to tackle poverty, housing, family planning. People are still multiplying.

Om   Toh, forget it.

Vishram (*noticing* **Om**'s *bandaged hand*)   What happened to you? Been in a fight?

Om   It's long story.

Vishram   So many modern *Mahabharatas* are spun out over a cup of my chai.

Om (*seeing* **Ishvar** *and* **Maneck**)   Chini jyada dalna and two more strong chai.

Om *offers* **Maneck** *a beedi, as he is smoking himself.*

Maneck   No thanks. I don't smoke.

Ishvar   So, detective sahib? Found out where Dinabai goes? Name of Mrs Gupta's company? Address?

Om   Have you tried following a taxi on a cycle?

Ishvar   Was it my crazy idea? So you shed your own blood for nothing?

Om   Don't maro such heavy dialogue.

Maneck   What did you do?

Om   Stabbed myself with scissors so Dinabai would let me see a doctor. How else could I get out of the house yaar to follow her to Mrs Gupta's? She locks us in.

Maneck   What?

Ishvar   To kya hua?

Om   I had the taxi well in my sight yaar, but then I had to keep changing lanes to keep up, and on the main road the taxi disappeared. There were so many of the same – same yellow and black Fiats with their meters sticking out . . . I didn't know which one to follow. I thought I had the right one just as I squeezed between two cars and was knocked off my bike.

Ishvar   Hai Bhagwan! Your anger will always lead to haste!

Om (*flashing fifty rupees*)   Well, my haste got me fifty rupees! (*To* **Maneck**.) We can go to movie. *Revolver Rani*.

Ishvar   Where from?

Om   Compensation from driver, but I got up too fast. I should have screamed and shouted that I was dying and done him for two hundred.

Ishvar   Only to you could such things happen. And if your finger goes septic and your tailoring is kaput? How long will your fifty rupees last?

Om   Ja ja. It's not that bad.

Maneck   Why do you need to know where Mrs Gupta lives?

Om   So we can talk directly to her instead of being fleeced.

Maneck   I'm sure Dina Auntie wouldn't do that.

Ishvar   You have better things to do than get involved in Om's sorry story. Like make your father proud with your studies.

Maneck   Even if I was A-grade student, it wouldn't make my father proud.

Om   Don't talk bakwaas.

Maneck   It's true. 'The slow coach always gets left behind' he's always saying. But he's the one who's the slow coach. He won't even change a packet of biscuits in his shop . . .

Ishvar   You have a shop?

Maneck   I hope to run it one day . . .

Om   Look, your father sent you here to study because he cares about your future.

Maneck   You're an expert on fathers or what?

Om   Yes.

Maneck   What makes you?

Om   Because my father is dead. That quickly makes you an expert. So stop talking rubbish about your father.

Maneck   Acha, acha. My father is a saint.

Om   I'm never going to be a father.

Maneck   Me neither.

Om   Maybe we should have the snip. Government is offering radio.

Ishvar   Don't even joke about such things. You will marry when I tell you. No arguments.

Om   Everyone has a radio.

Ishvar   Everyone jumps in the well? You will also? Learning big city ways.

Om   You get the operation if you don't want me to.

Ishvar   Shameless! My manhood for a stupid radio?

Om   Who are you saving your manhood for?

Ishvar (*meaning he has sacrificed himself for* **Om**)   Who have I sacrificed myself for?

Silence as this hits home to **Om**.

Ishvar   You want transistor? Get back to work and save.

They get up to go.

Om   Put it on the tab.

As they leave, they see **Woman** *washing and drying half her sari.*

Om   You see that woman? She's always at the pump. She has only one sari.

Scene Five

Dina*'s flat.*

The tailors and **Maneck** *come back from the restaurant and go to* **Dina***'s flat.*

Dina (*to* **Om**)   So how far was your doctor? The southernmost tip of Lanka?

Om   Yes. I was carried through the sky by Lord Hanuman.

Dina   This fellow is getting very sharp.

They get back to their sewing.

Dina (*to* **Maneck**)   Were you smoking with these two?

Maneck   No, Auntie.

Dina   Under my roof, I stand in your parents' place.

Maneck   They were smoking and I was sitting next to them.

Dina (*to the tailors*)   You shouldn't smoke. Cancer will eat your lungs.

Om   This expensive city will eat us alive before that.

Dina   Work hard and you'll earn plenty of money.

Om (*under his breath*)   Not the way you pay us.

Dina   Did you say something?

Om   Do you have to go far to get the work?

Dina   Not far.

Om   And what is the name of the company you go to?

Dina   Why you bother with the name? All I'm concerned is that the work gets done.

Ishvar   And that is what interests us also.

They start sewing.

Dina (*to* **Om**)   The seams from yesterday weren't straight.

Ishvar   I will separate them and do them again.

Dina   He makes mistakes. He should correct them.

Om   You can hardly see in this dim light.

Dina   If I exceed the monthly quota, my meter will be disconnected. Then we'll be in total darkness.

Ishvar   Shall we move the Singers to the front room?

Dina   And parade yourself to the whole street? The landlord will accuse me of running a factory from my flat.

Om   So you lock us in when you go out so no one can see us.

Dina   I have no choice.

Om   You think we're thieves.

Ishvar   She's not saying that . . .

Om   We're going to take your possessions and run away.

Dina   The landlord could barge in and throw you out on the street. But he wouldn't dare to break the padlock. It's against the law.

They sew some more.

Om   Very difficult pattern. We'll have to charge more this time for sure.

Dina   For the commission I get on the order, I pay you a fair rate. So stop your khutt khutt and get to work. And take your fingers out of your hair before you get oil on the cloth. Scratch, scratch, scratch the whole day.

Dina *moves off and* **Ishvar** *approaches her.*

Ishvar   Om is not a bad boy. If sometimes he's disobedient or bad-tempered, it's only because he's frustrated and unhappy. He has had a very unfortunate life.

Dina   You think mine has been easy? But we must make the best of what we have.

Ishvar   May I take some water from the kitchen?

Dina   Use the plain glasses. The frosted ones are for Maneck and me.

Ishvar *goes to the kitchen.* **Om** *indicates for* **Maneck** *to come over.*

Om   Not having a husband makes her sour. She needs someone to service her.

Maneck   Don't talk about Dina Auntie like that.

Om   But it's true. If she had a man . . .

Maneck   Mummy says the way she loved her husband, she could never look at another man.

Om   Doesn't stop us looking at her.

Maneck   Stop it.

Om   Ever done it?

Maneck   Almost. On a railway train.

Om   You're a champion fakeologist, for sure. On a train!

Maneck   No, really. A few months ago, when I left home to come to college. There was a woman in the upper booth, opposite mine. Very beautiful.

Om   More beautiful than Dinabai?

Maneck   No. But the minute I got on the train, she kept staring at me, smiling when no one was watching. The problem was, her father was travelling with her. Finally night came and people began going to sleep. She and I kept awake. When everyone had fallen asleep, she pushed aside the sheet and pulled one breast out from her choli.

Om   Then what?

Maneck   She began massaging her breast and signalled for me to come over. I was scared to climb down from my berth. But then she put her hand between her legs and began rubbing herself. So I decided I had to go to her.

Om   Of course, you'd be a fool not to.

Maneck   I got down without disturbing anyone. She grabbed my hand, begging me to climb in with her. Just as I wondered the best way to get up there, her father turned over in the berth underneath, groaning. She was so frightened that she pushed me away and started snoring loudly. If only the bastard had kept sleeping.

Om   Shit, yah.

Maneck   It's so sad. I'll never meet that woman again.

During this **Ishvar** *has returned and started working again. The siren sounds indicating that it's six o'clock.*

Om   It's six o'clock.

They pack up to go.

Dina   Tomorrow order has to be finished. So don't be late like today.

Ishvar   There was an accident. Train was delayed.

Dina   Under the Emergency, government says railways run on time. Strange that your train keeps coming late.

Ishvar   You can't trust the government.

They go.

Maneck   Why do you fight with them, Auntie?

Dina   You dare to ask me? Do you know the whole story?

Maneck   I'm sorry, Auntie. I meant . . .

Dina   Mistakes and shoddy work. But thank God for Ishvar. One angel and one devil. Trouble is when Angel keeps company with the Devil, neither can be trusted.

Maneck   Do you really lock them in?

Dina   The landlord's threat is real – you remember it too. Always pretend you're my nephew.

Maneck *doesn't say anything.*

Dina   I'm telling you. If I don't lock them in, they could go outside and blab to the world that they're working here. Then what would happen? As it is I can barely manage. My tiny commission sticks in their throat.

Maneck   Shall I tell Mummy to send more money?

Dina   Absolutely not.

Maneck   For my rent and food?

Dina   I'm charging a fair price and she's paying it. If I wanted charity I could have played the poor widow and languished at my brother's.

Scene Six

Clearing of the slums.

The tailors are back in the slums

Om   I'm starving.

Ishvar   Do you have worms? Now if you were married, your wife would have food cooked and waiting for you.

Om   Why don't you get married? I've selected a wife for you.

Ishvar   Who?

Om   Dinabai. I know you like her, you're always taking her side. You should give her a poke.

Ishvar   Shameless boy!

The rumbling sounds of a bulldozer coming closer. Announcements on the loudspeaker:

Announcement　Keep back! These slums are illegal. Beautification police! We have orders to destroy the huts! Piche hato!

Om　Hai Ram! What is going on?

Rajaram *comes running on as the slums are cleared.*

Rajaram　Run! Run! They are clearing people also.

Announcement　Collect your belongings and move on or you will be moved!

The slums are completely demolished. Slum-dwellers grab what belongings they can, and flee. The bulldozers come in and flatten the place. The dust settles.

Time passes. **Monkeyman** *comes on and starts to make a shrine. He puts on top a garlanded picture of Leila the monkey and Tikka the dog. He speaks to Tikka, cajoling him to come over.*

Monkeyman　Aaja, Tikka, aaja . . . In one day how our fortunes changed! While I showered rose petals on Mother India at rally, she had our homes flattened by bulldozer . . . all crooks and liars. While I ate free bhajia, you were so hungry you had to bite into your own sister. She is also gone . . . beloved to God . . . only two of us left . . . Never mind I forgive you . . . You played like children, I thought she was safe but Dog is dumb animal, I should have known . . . all my fault for leaving you alone . . . Come . . . aaja eat Prasad. Offering to the gods . . . Look what I got . . . lovely picture of you with your monkey sister on your back when she still alive, before you became Badmash. All family was together . . . Kodak moment taken by that American tourist. He enjoyed our act. yaad he? Sister, you and Papa. Come fold your hands and pray for sister's soul . . . aaja . . . mourn with me, then we have special treat. I got five rupees from rally.

Tikka comes over and **Monkeyman** *slits his throat.*

Now your sinners soul is free, like your innocent sister's.

Scene Seven

Au Revoir Exports.

Mrs Gupta comes on with a bouffant hairdo. She greets **Dina***.*

Mrs Gupta   Hello, Mrs Dalal. I've just been at the hair salon. What do you think?

Dina   Beautiful.

Mrs Gupta   It's a bouffant.

Dina   It sets off your cheekbones.

Mrs Gupta   Stop, you are making me blush. Empty-handed? Where is my order?

Dina   My tailors haven't come for a few days.

Mrs Gupta   That's very inconvenient. Where are they?

Dina (*lying*)   They had a bereavement in the family.

Mrs Gupta   Drinking and dancing in their village, no doubt. Too many production days are lost with such excuses. When will they be back?

Dina   Soon I hope.

Mrs Gupta   We are third-world in development but first-class in absenteeism and strikes. The Emergency is good medicine for the nation. I'm with Mrs Gandhi on this.

Dina   Surely she only declared Emergency because the court found her guilty of cheating in the election.

Mrs Gupta   No, no, no! That is all rubbish, it will be appealed. Now all these troublemakers who accused her falsely have been put in jail.

Dina   Seems like anyone can be in jail these days for no rhyme or reason.

Mrs Gupta   What nonsense, Mrs Dalal!

Dina   They are overflowing the jails with MISA suspects and holding them without trial.

Mrs Gupta   What do you know about Maintenance of Internal Security when you don't even know where your tailors are?

Dina   Maneck tells me of daily arrests on his campus. Anyone who speaks out against the Emergency is a target.

Mrs Gupta   So your adolescent boarder from the mountains is informing your politics? What does he know about the real threats to this country? Laziness and indiscipline! Indiscipline is the mother of chaos. The need of the hour is discipline and that is the Prime Minister's message on the posters, which I have hung prominently for all my workers to see.

Dina   Yes, Mrs Gupta.

Mrs Gupta   Now, about my order.

Dina   I am sure the tailors will be back soon.

Mrs Gupta   No more delays, Mrs Dalal. Remember, strict rules and firm supervision leads to success. Tailors are very strange people. They work with tiny needles but strut about as if they are carrying big swords. You must keep control.

Dina   Han.

Mrs Gupta   You are the boss. I don't give my workers rest. Rest causes thinking and thinking causes excuses. I don't allow it. You must have workers, not shirkers. This is why I'm a big businesswoman and Mr Gupta can sit at home in his slippers. My exporters rely on me. 'Mrs Gupta,' they say, 'you are simply marvellous. Always on time.' Highly prestigious labels from America and Europe are asking for my creations. In just one year I have doubled my turnover at Au Revoir Exports. Make sure your tailors are back – if your order is not in by next Friday, I will have to bid you *au revoir*.

Dina   Yes, Friday, then.

Scene Eight

The building site to which **Om** *and* **Ishvar** *have been cleared. Workers are breaking stones and making gravel.* **Ishvar** *half-fills a woman's basket.*

Woman 1   Fill it to the top.

Ishvar   I have never done this work before.

Woman 1   Filling is easy. (*Getting up.*) For carrying, you need balance.

Ishvar   The heat is making me feel faint.

Woman 2   No sympathy here, bachu!

Woman 1   Water is coming.

Om *wets his hair with his spit and puts a comb through it.*

Woman 2   Oh hero ke bache! Get back to work or overseer will have something to say.

Om   We're tailors, not stone-breakers.

Woman 2   And I'm the Queen of Jhansi.

Ishvar   There is a mistake. We shouldn't be here.

Man 1   Couldn't agree more, nimble fingers!

Man 2   Homeless amateurs they round up!

Ishvar   We are not homeless, they destroyed our homes!

Shankar *comes with water and gives it to the thirsty workers.*

Man 1 (*about* **Shankar**)   And this beggar? What kind of labourer is he going to make?

Woman 1   Chup kur! At least he quenches your thirst.

She drinks and exits during the following lines.

Shankar   Arey babu! Without beggars how will people wash away their sins?

Man 2   Listen to him! Holier than thou!

Woman 2   Suer ka bacha! Give me some water.

Shankar *goes up to the tailors and talks to them.*

Shankar   They don't like us here.

Ishvar   Because they think we are after their livelihood.

Shankar   Little do they know my livelihood would put their meagre wages to shame. I command the city's top begging spots. Office crowd, lunch crowd, shopping crowd . . . such takings!

Ishvar   What bad kismet that we got cleared away. At least we are together.

Shankar   Han. I wish my Beggarmaster would come and find me.

Om   You think he's looking?

Ishvar   We need to get out of here.

The siren sounds. **Shankar** *exits and everyone lies down to rest.*

Scene Nine

Split focus on stage:

Workers asleep on the building site.

Dina's *flat.*

Dina *comes on with stacks of cloth for an order. The doorbell rings.*

Dina (*to* **Maneck**, *who is off*)   It's Ibrahim, Maneck – stay hidden.

There is a familiarity to this drill. **Dina** *gets an envelope out of one of the machine drawers and goes to let* **Ibrahim** *in. He greets her as she hands him an envelope*

Ibrahim   Adab, sister!

Dina   Please count it.

Ibrahim   No need, sister. Twenty-year tenant like you. If I can't trust you, who can I trust?

He fumbles with his folder and elastic band.

Please, sister, can I sit for a minute to find your receipt, or everything will fall to the ground? Old hands are clumsy hands. Lucky legs are still working.

He sits and surveys the room. He clocks the sewing machines.

Ibrahim   You have two Singers in this room?

Dina   There's no law against two machines, is there?

Ibrahim   Not at all, just asking. Although with this crazy Emergency, you can never tell what law there is. The government surprises us daily.

Dina   One has a light needle, the other heavy. Presser-feet and tensions are also different.

Ibrahim   They look exactly the same to me, but what do I know about sewing? . . . So where does the young man live?

Dina   What?

Ibrahim   The young man, sister. Your paying guest.

Dina   How dare you suggest I keep young men in my flat?

Ibrahim   Please. That's not what I . . .

Dina   Haven't you got enough adulterers to blackmail? You want to sully a defenceless widow's reputation?

Ibrahim   Forgive me, sister. Must be a silly rumour.

Dina   If there's nothing else, I will see you next month.

Ibrahim   With your permission, sister. Your humble servant.

He leaves and **Maneck** *comes back in.*

Maneck   Sorry, Auntie. You shouldn't have to listen to that.

Dina   Can't be helped.

Maneck   At least rent is paid up and water and electricity too.

Dina   We can't eat electricity. No sign of those buggers! How will I deliver my order? If they don't turn up, I'll have to go cap in hand to my brother.

Maneck   Auntie, Vishram at the tea stall told me Om and Ishvar's homes were destroyed and they were dragged into the police truck. God knows where they are now. In jail?

Dina   And how long is their sentence? One week? Two? If those rascals were moonlighting somewhere else this would be the way to do it, starting a rumour.

Maneck   It's not just them, Auntie. Everyone from the streets and slums, all the beggars and pavement-dwellers, were taken away by the police.

Dina   Surely there's no law for doing that.

Maneck   It's a new policy. City Beautification Plan or something, under the Emergency.

Dina   I am sick and tired of that stupid word.

Maneck   We could check with the police.

Dina   You think they will unlock the jail on my say-so?

Maneck   At least we would know where they are.

Dina   At this moment, I'm more worried about these dresses.

Maneck   I knew it. You're so selfish, you don't think about anyone but yourself.

Dina   How dare you talk to me like that?

Maneck   Om and Ishvar could be dead for all you care.

He goes off and slams the door.

Dina   If you damage my door, I'll send you back express delivery to your parents.

Maneck *comes back out.*

Maneck   When do you have to deliver them?

Dina   Day after tomorrow. By twelve o'clock.

Maneck   That's two whole days. Lots of time.

Dina   For two expert tailors. Not for me alone.

Maneck   I'll help you.

Dina   But there are sixty dresses. Six-zero. Hems and buttons all to be done by hand.

Maneck   How will they know if we do it by machine?

Dina   The difference is like night and day.

Maneck   We have forty-eight hours till delivery time.

Dina   If we don't eat or sleep or go to the bathroom.

Maneck   We can at least try. Deliver what we finish and make an excuse that the tailors fell sick or something.

Dina   You're a good boy, you know. Your parents are very fortunate.

Maneck   That must be why they sent me away.

Dina   They want you to have a better life than theirs.

Maneck   My life was perfect before my father sent me to boarding school and now here.

Dina   You not happy here?

Maneck   No . . . no . . . Dina Auntie, I didn't mean . . . Come on, Auntie . . . let's give it a go!

Dina   What about college?

Maneck   No lectures today.

Dina   Come, I'll teach you buttons. Easier than hems.

Maneck   Anything. I learn quickly.

He threads a needle and puts it in his mouth.

Dina   Take it out at once before you swallow it.

Maneck   You never shout at Om for doing that.

Dina   That's different. He's trained. He grew up with tailors.

Maneck   No, he didn't. His family used to be cobblers.

Dina   And you know so much about them?

Maneck   Om told me.

Dina   You should keep your distance.

Maneck   You want me to treat them like they got treated in their village? They were . . . leather workers. Untouchable. Spat on by the landowners . . .

Dina   These Hindus and their outdated caste system.

Maneck   Om told me in confidence. They were scared of being treated badly if anyone knew.

Dina   You can tell me. I don't believe in these customs.

Maneck   Auntie, you have no idea.

Dina   And you do?

Maneck   You know Om's father and Ishvar were caned as children for daring to touch the chalks and slates in the village school. So their father then decided he didn't want his sons to be slaves to the upper castes. He sent them to become apprentices with his Muslim tailor friend in the city – Ashraf. When Om's dad came back to the village, he was successful and the high castes didn't like it. When he went to cast his vote in the village election, the landowner Thakur Dharamsi took his revenge on the whole family.

Dina   What did he do?

Maneck   They hung Om's dad from a banyan tree and the rest of the family were torched.

Dina   Oh my God!

Maneck   Om and Ishvar only survived because they were with Ashraf in the city.

Dina   Such horrible suffering! I had no idea . . . Day after day they sat quietly working without saying a word and to you they tell their life story.

Maneck Maybe they were afraid of you?

Dina Afraid of me? What nonsense. If anything I was afraid of them. That they would find Mrs Gupta's company and cut me out or get better jobs. Sometimes I was afraid even to point out their mistakes. I would correct them at night after they left. God only knows where they are.

Scene Ten

Split stage:

The building site, where people are still resting. **Om** *and* **Ishvar** *are restless.*

Dina *in her flat, sewing.*

Ishvar Dresses will be late again. What will Dinabai do?

Om Find new tailors and forget about us. What else? We should never have come to the city. We could've stayed being Ashraf chacha's apprentices.

Ishvar Ashraf chacha couldn't afford to keep us any more. Ready-made clothes ruined his business. As it is, I'll always be grateful we were safe with him or we would have perished with the rest of our family in the village.

Om I wish I had died with them.

Ishvar Don't ever say that.

Om Why not? Why were we spared, Uncle? Why?

Ishvar To make a better future.

Om What future? God is having a joke. Letting us train as tailors only to toil to death in this hell of heartless devils.

Ishvar It's not God. It is this Emergency. You must have hope.

Om Like my father had when he trained with Ashraf chacha and came back to the village?

Ishvar   It was his pride, not his hope, that came before a fall. You can't walk tall in front of the upper castes.

Om   So you lower your eyes to the ground and live a long life?

Ishvar   What do you know? Born yesterday. What do you know about the endurance of your people? The timeless chain of caste that shackled us to work with carcasses and filth while being treated worse than animals. It was my father who dared to break the chain by sending me and my brother to train as tailors. Yes, he lowered his eyes and waited for the seed of hope he sowed to grow. But your father was impatient, wanting change overnight and I see that streak in you.

Om   He went to cast his vote, which is every man's right.

Ishvar   For us rights and wrongs are determined by the likes of Thakur Dharamsi. Be grateful our caste is invisible in the city. We will get out of here, work hard, get you married. You must continue our bloodline and who knows what your children will become?

Shankar *rolls in on his platform with food, balancing the dinner slowly and carefully. He offers it to the tailors.*

Shankar   Eat, it will give you strength. Chew properly. No rushing.

The tailors start eating. Again **Ishvar** *puts some of his food on* **Om***'s plate without him noticing.*

Shankar   More chappatis? I made friends with someone in the kitchen. I can get as many as I like.

Ishvar   No, Worm . . . bas.

Shankar *starts to leave the site.*

Om   Any news from your Beggarmaster?

Shankar   He will think I have run away when he comes to my pavement spot tomorrow for my money.

Ishvar   If he asks around, someone will tell him the police took you.

Shankar   That's what I still can't understand. Why did the police take me? Beggarmaster pays them every week. All his beggars are allowed to work without harassment.

Ishvar   These are different police. Beautification police.

Om   Ugly bastards!

Ishvar   Maybe they don't know your Beggarmaster.

Shankar   Arey! Everybody knows Beggarmaster.

Om   With his briefcase handcuffed to his hand, he looks like underworld gangster.

Shankar   Gangster only to his enemies, to his aapne he is like God. He looks after my everything. When I was little, he carried me around and used to rent me out each day. I was in great demand. I earned him the highest profits. A child, a suckling cripple, earns a lot of money from the public. Wish I could still be carried around in women's arms, their sweet nipples in my mouth. Better than bumping along all day on this platform, banging my balls and wearing out my buttocks.

Ishvar   Your life is hard.

Shankar   But the rewards were sweet. If I was good, Beggarmaster took me to a prostitute. Especially on my birthday. Now I feel all alone. I want to go home!

Ishvar   Have faith.

Shankar *leaves.*

Om   If you hear from your Beggarmaster, put in a word for us as well . . . get us out of here.

Scene Eleven

A bedraggled and forlorn **Monkeyman** *comes on with the* **Woman** *from the slum. A melancholic Hindi song is heard played on an accordion.*

Monkeyman   This world is Maya, isn't it, ladies and gentlemen? . . . All illusion. One day you have a home and the next it has disappeared into thin air! Even this body that houses a soul is temporary.

Woman   We are but travellers in this journey that is life.

Monkeyman *starts drumming.*

Monkeyman   Now throw your money and you will see real tamasha. You won't believe your eyes! How much will you give? (*Looking around the audience and negotiating.*) Five rupees? For five rupees you get two-paisa snake-charmer. Where's the thrill? Did I hear ten rupee? When I had monkey, you could have show for ten rupee. Even that was cheap, hena?

Woman   Han.

Monkeyman   I am looking for twenty rupee. Only twenty rupee for exclusive show? Never seen before. Bargain. Only for you. (*Spotting someone.*) I have twenty rupee here. Thank you. Shall we accept?

Woman *accepts.*

Woman   You help the poor. May God bless you and give you moksha so you are never reborn on this wretched earth.

Monkeyman   Come closer, Dekho. Come see . . . This will take your breath away. Ladies and gentlemen, my niece Chunni! You want to do trick? Chunni is going to do trick for you.

Woman *brings* **Chunni** *forward. The little girl is shy.*

Monkeyman   She is so shy. So beautiful. So salaam beta. Public want to see your pretty face.

The girl greets the audience. **Monkeyman** *and* **Woman** *tie her up to a pole.*

Monkeyman   Shabash. Good girl. She is only small, but soon we will make her tall. She will reach the stars. Round and round she goes . . . she will reach the heavens.

Monkeyman *brings the girl down, and* **Woman** *starts to untie her.*

Monkeyman   What's wrong? She enjoys it. Like being on a merry-go-round. You call me badmash?

Woman   Raen de.

Monkeyman   He call me villian. Everyone has to make a living . . . you pay me now.

Woman   Leave it.

Monkeyman   You pay me . . . We agreed.

Woman   Let's go. They didn't appreciate . . .

Monkeyman   You think I like?

He picks up and cradles his niece.

What to do now my Leila is gone? My Leila would play bride, her face hidden under a beautiful veil. How she would cry like real bride leaving her father's house for the last time . . .

Woman (*singing*)   'Babul ki duaen leti jaa' . . .

Monkeyman   She left me for ever and it is me who is crying.

Woman   Bus. Come on.

Monkeyman *walks off.*

Woman   He is not the same since monkey passed away. Some say he used to do dirty things with her. Who's to say? Everyone needs comfort. Little does he know. I have seen a prophecy. The loss of the monkey is not the worst loss he will suffer. The murder of the dog is not the worst murder he'll commit.

Scene Twelve

Nusswan's *office.*

Nusswan *presses his bell for* **Dina** *to come in.* **Dina** *and* **Maneck** *enter.*

Dina   You're turning European? Usually you make me wait at least fifteen minutes.

Nusswan   Well, I am free. Usually I'm busy.

Dina   How are Ruby and the boys?

Nusswan   They are well. Not that Xerxes and Zarir are boys any more. Older than this young man, I should imagine. You've missed their childhood.

Dina   Where are my manners? This is Maneck. Maneck, this is my brother Nusswan.

Nusswan   Pleased to meet you.

Maneck   Lovely to meet you.

Dina   Maneck has heard a lot about you from me, and I wanted the two of you to meet. He came to live with me a few months ago.

Nusswan   Live with you?

Dina   What else would a paying guest do?

Nusswan   Yes, yes, of course. But your flat is the size of a matchbox. And what with tailors and sewing machines, where has she put you?

Maneck   Em . . .

Dina   He's in my room and I sleep with the sewing machines.

Nusswan   Dina, Dina! I ask you, is this independence? (*To* **Maneck**.) She had a home. With us.

Dina   I couldn't live off your charity for ever.

Nusswan   What charity? It was quid pro quo. You could have carried on making yourself useful to Ruby.

Dina   Like a servant. You let go of the servant.

Nusswan   So, Maneck, where do you work?

Dina   Work? He's just seventeen. He goes to college.

Nusswan   And what are you studying?

Maneck   Refrigeration and air-conditioning.

Nusswan   Very wise choice. The future lies with technology and modernisation. Magnificent changes are taking place in this country. And the credit goes to our Prime Minister. Thanks to our visionary leader and her beautification programme, this city will be restored to its former glory

Dina   Well, in this beautification I have lost my tailors.

Nusswan   What a pity.

Dina   They were an eyesore, so were carted off by the police somewhere.

Nusswan   Well. poverty has to be tackled head on. Mrs Gandhi's twenty-point programme has pragmatic policies, not irrelevant theories. A good friend of mine was saying only last week – and he's the director of a multinational, mind, not some two paisa home-grown business, Maneck – he was saying that at least two hundred million people are surplus to requirement, they should be eliminated.

Maneck   Eliminated?

Nusswan   Yes. You know – got rid of . . .

Maneck   But how would they be eliminated?

Nusswan   That's easy. Feed them a free meal of arsenic or cyanide. Lorries could go around to the temples and places where they gather to beg. Counting them as unemployment statistics year after year just makes the numbers look bad. And what are their lives? Sitting in the gutter. Looking like corpses. Death would be a mercy. So what can I do for you, little sister?

Dina   Until I find new tailors, I can't accept any more orders.

Nusswan (*to* **Maneck**)   Could you excuse us? My peon will get you a tea.

Maneck   Yes, of course.

He exits.

Nusswan   What are you doing? Cavorting around with students less than half your age? You think you're in Hollywood? Rubbing my nose in it.

Dina   How am I rubbing your nose?

Nusswan   With your defiance and dis—

Dina   Disobedience?! I'm not a kid.

Nusswan   As if you listened to me, then. Scoffing at my authority with your accusing eyes.

Dina   Who made me Sellotape my pigtails back on my head as punishment for getting a bob?

Nusswan   You know what community is saying about you?

Dina   You can revel in their sympathy. 'Poor Nusswan, can't tame his unruly sister.'

Nusswan   How much is that boarder paying you?

Dina   Maneck. You want to know all my credits and debits before you agree to help me?

Nusswan   Have I ever refused you? Even when you married that unambitious medicine-mixing fool.

Dina   Whatever happened to not speaking ill of the dead?

Nusswan   What was wrong with Poros? Or Solly?

Dina   If you discount the pot belly. Nothing.

Nusswan   Pot belly, he's got only now. Sign of prosperity. And your Rustom. Unfortunate in looks, unfortunate in money and unfortunate in life span. What you saw in him? Poetry and recitals! Since when did Bach pay the bills? Fiancés buy diamonds as an engagement present – a brooch. When he came in with that pagoda-green umbrella –

Dina   He didn't want me to get wet . . .

Nusswan   – still I supported your decision. What a lavish wedding I gave you. Forty-eight guests, caterers and bottles of Johnnie Walker.

Dina   Which you and your friends consumed.

Nusswan   Talking of friends, Jehangir would have had you, even after being widowed.

Dina   If I wanted to marry again, I am sure I could promenade on the parade even now with a sign around my neck and someone would take pity on me.

Nusswan   You were beautiful, Dina. Still not bad, considering your age. You could have lived like a queen!

Dina   I could have gone to the Towers of Silence and let the vultures eat me alive!

Nusswan   Such blasphemy! Khudaya! What would our father in heaven say?

He fills out a cash voucher.

Give this to the cashier.

Dina   I always pay you back.

Nusswan   And remember. My door is always open.

Scene Thirteen

Om, **Shankar** *and* **Ishvar** *are in a truck with* **Beggarmaster**, *heading back to the city at night.*

Om   Look. People are sleeping peacefully. No police to bother them. Maybe the Emergency has been cancelled.

Beggarmaster   No, it has become a game, like all the other laws. Easy to play, once you know the rules. Since you are Worm's friends, I am willing to help you.

Ishvar   We are very grateful to you for securing our release from the irrigation project.

Beggarmaster   Gratitude is good. Do you have any experience?

Ishvar   Oh yes, many years' experience.

Beggarmaster   It doesn't look to me that you could be successful.

Om   We are fully trained. We can even take measurements straight from the customer's body.

Beggarmaster   Measurements from the body?

Om   Of course. We are skilled tailors, not hacks.

Beggarmaster   I thought you wanted to work for me as beggars. I have no need for tailors. I'll take you back to the site.

Ishvar   No, please, Beggarmaster, there must be some other way to show our gratitude.

Beggarmaster   Usually when I look after a beggar, I charge one hundred rupees a week – begging space, food, clothes, protection all inclusive.

Ishvar   Yes, Shankar . . . Worm told us about it.

Shankar   You are a very kind Beggarmaster. I knew you will find me.

Beggarmaster   I can't afford to lose you.

Ishvar   What luck for all of us that you came to the rescue.

Beggarmaster   Luck has little to do with it. I am the most famous Beggarmaster in the city.

Ishvar   We know.

Beggarmaster   Anyway, your case is different, you don't need looking after in the same way. Just pay me fifty a week per person, for one year.

Om   That's almost two thousand five hundred each.

Beggarmaster   It's minimum for what I'm offering.

Ishvar   Three days' worth of sewing each week. We won't be able to afford it. We'll give you twenty-five.

Beggarmaster   I'm not selling onions and potatoes in the bazaar. My business is looking after human lives. Don't try to bargain with me

Ishvar   We'll take it.

Beggarmaster   What's your credentials? How will I know you can pay?

Shankar   They have good jobs with a Parsi lady.

Beggarmaster   I will have to verify it for myself when I drop you off.

Ishvar   No, no . . . We can't disturb Dinabai in the middle of the night.

Om   She is bad-tempered. We will surely lose our jobs.

Beggarmaster   Then there's always Plan B. Begging for me. Although we'll have to arrange some injuries.

Om and **Ishvar** *are horrified.*

Ishvar   Don't worry, we will introduce you to Dinabai.

Beggarmaster   I'll come personally every Thursday to collect my weekly payment.

Ishvar   Haanji.

Beggarmaster   Sometimes one of my clients will vanish without paying, after enjoying my hospitality. But I always manage to find them. Please remember that.

Scene Fourteen

Dina *lays out the table for four with* **Maneck** *helping her. A record of Bob Dylan singing can be heard from the upstairs flat.*

Dina   Those hippies upstairs and their love affair with Bob Dylan.

Maneck   It's kind of you to ask Om and Ishvar to eat with us.

Dina   It's practical. If they are under my roof they won't disappear into the wilderness. I have to rebuild my credibility with Mrs Gupta.

Maneck   You've used your best plates.

Dina   No point keeping fine china for fancy occasions that never arise.

Pause.

The last time all the sides of this table were occupied was my third wedding anniversary – the night Rustom was killed. He just popped out on his bicycle to get vanilla ice cream for Nusswan's boys. It was raining . . . I made tea . . . He should have been ten minutes. I put a tea-cosy over the pot. Still it went cold. He never came back. It was a hit-and-run.

Maneck   Mummy told me. What a tragic accident.

Dina   The policeman said a stray dog lapped up the thick pink puddle of ice cream that fell from his hands. They didn't have vanilla, he must've got strawberry not to disappoint the children. Sometimes, from the verandah, I still imagine him peddling in the distance.

She calls the tailors to the table.

Khana table pe lag gaya he.

She goes back in.

Ishvar   She's calling us to the table.

Om   So we should go.

Ishvar *and* **Om** *tentatively take their places at the table. They look nervously at the cutlery and proceed to eat with their hands.* **Dina** *and* **Maneck** *realise they are not comfortable with cutlery; they put their own cutlery down and also eat with their hands.* **Ishvar** *can't contain himself. He breaks down.*

Ishvar   Oh, Dinabai, I don't know how to thank you. Such kindness! We are so afraid of the outside . . . this Emergency, the police. We didn't know where we were. I thought we would die on that irrigation project. I don't know how to thank you.

Dina   Bus karo, please. There is no need for all this.

Ishvar   I just don't know how to thank you

Dina   There have been enough thanks for one day. Now eat.

They eat.

I don't like you getting in the clutches of this Beggarmaster fellow. He sounds fearsome.

Ishvar   Better the devil you know, Dinabai.

They eat. **Om** *scratches his head.*

Dina   We will have to put some kerosene on that hair.

Om   Does it poison the lice?

Maneck   I'll tell you.

Om   You are a champion fakeologist.

Maneck   Listen. First every louse soaks itself in kerosene. In the middle of the night when you are asleep, Dina Auntie gives each one a tiny matchstick. At the count of three they commit suicide in bursts of tiny flames without hurting you. There'll be a beautiful halo around your head when it happens.

Dina   That's not funny, Mac.

Om   Mac?

Maneck   My nickname. I hate it.

Ishvar   Thank you, Dinabai, for letting us sleep on the verandah last night.

Dina   Where else would you have gone?

Ishvar   Can we leave our trunk here?

Dina   Where will you sleep tonight?

Ishvar   I don't know. Maybe we'll find some doorway of a shop. Even for that you have to grease someone's palm.

Dina   You can stay here.

Ishvar   Thank you. And we will pay.

Dina   Absolutely no rent. Ibrahim will have me for subletting. Just keeping you out of those crooked police hands.

Maneck (*aside*)   I'm very proud of you, Dina Auntie.

There is a knock at the door. **Maneck** *goes and ushers* **Rajaram** *in.*

Dina   This fellow came before also. Says he's your friend.

Ishvar   Rajaram!

Dina   So you know him?

Ishvar   He showed us great kindness when we first came to the city.

Dina   Please talk to him on the verandah.

As the tailors talk to **Rajaram,** **Dina** *takes up sewing*

Ishvar   Where did you disappear to?

Rajaram   When the bulldozers came, I thought you two were kaput. Where have you been?

Om   VIP guests of Mrs Gandhi's.

Rajaram   In the lock-up?

Ishvar   We were rounded up and forced to work as muzdurs on irrigation project.

Rajaram (*to* **Om**)   You lost weight.

Om   Special government diet.

Rajaram   Still got your sense of humour.

Ishvar   Kya kahen? Our kismet has dragged us every which way and now we are back at Dinabai's.

Rajaram   Lucky you! You're onto a good wicket here, I see. You were right about her hair.

Ishvar   Look, you can't stay long.

Rajaram   I have a problem, only a small obstacle but with my profession I need storage space.

Ishvar   For what?

Rajaram   Currently I'm specialising in plaits, but sleeping on the streets I have nowhere to store what I collect. Will you keep it safe for me? Your good friend?

Om   We have our trunk.

Rajaram *hands over a bag.* **Om** *takes out two exuberant plaits and starts fingering them.*

Rajaram   Don't touch them!

Om   Sorry yaar.

Rajaram   No no! It's just the hair-agents are fussy about clean hair.

Om   I wash my hands with Lifebuoy. How did you get these two? So cleanly cropped.

Rajaram   They wanted pageboy-style.

Ishvar   You cutting hair again?

Rajaram   Mostly pavement-barbering. Just to keep me going. So you'll keep this safe?

Ishvar   As safe as anything is these days.

Rajaram   Thank you, and if I want to add more I can always come here?

Ishvar   Nahin nahin, you'll scare Dinabai. As it is, she thinks we're mixing with crooks and crackpots. You just give it in a bag to Worm.

Om   That beggar with the gaadi. His patch is near that Vishram tea stall. He can be the go-between.

Rajaram   That beggar is your friend? Strange friends you make.

Ishvar   Yes. Very strange.

Rajaram   I won't forget this.

He exits. The tailors go back to where **Dina** *is sewing her quilt.*

Ishvar   Sorry, Dinabai.

Dina   You receive your visitors on the verandah. Strictly outside work hours.

Ishvar   No no, Dinabai, he won't disturb you again. He will meet us at the tea stall.

Dina   I was thinking. Make your tea here. Saves time.

Om (*about the quilt*)   What's this?

Dina   Maneck and I started a quilt. To pass the time when you were away.

Ishvar   It's good to use up the remnants and leftovers.

Om   But it's never cold in this city.

Ishvar   I remember that poplin, from our first job.

Dina   How fast you finished those dresses. I thought I had found two geniuses.

Maneck   And these blue and white flowers. You made these skirts the day I had my exams.

Om   And this. Our home was destroyed by the government, the day we started on this cloth.

Another knock at the door.

Dina   Who's there?

Ibrahim   Sorry to bother you, sister. But the office has sent me.

Dina   Couldn't it wait till morning?

Ibrahim   They said it was urgent, sister. I do as I'm told.

Ibrahim *enters with a* **Goonda**.

Dina   You can't just barge in.

Ibrahim   When you are using for commercial purposes, not domestic, the landlord has right of entry.

Dina   So why doesn't he come himself instead of sending his spy and stooge? I pay my rent, I'm entitled to privacy.

Ibrahim   It's not about rent. Office has sent me to deliver final notice – orally. Listen carefully. You must vacate in forty-eight hours. For violating terms and conditions.

Dina   I'm calling the police right now if you don't take your goonda and leave. If landlord has a problem, tell him I'll see him in court.

Ibrahim (*getting his folder out*)   It's all here . . . Dates, times, comings, goings, taxis, dresses – and these Singers are proof.

Dina   Proof of what?

Ibrahim   The problem is you cannot hire tailors and run business. And a paying guest. Insanity, sister.

Dina   Well, this is my husband and these two boys are our sons. Go tell your landlord.

Ibrahim   Marriage licence? Birth certificates? Can I see, please?

Dina   The back of my slipper across your mouth is what you'll see.

Ibrahim   Don't provoke desperate measures, sister.

Dina   You always get my money.

The **Goonda** *starts destroying her flat.*

Om   Bhenchod. If you're such a man, do your own dirty work.

Dina   Ishvar, run to the corner. Fetch the police.

The **Goonda** *stops him.*

Ibrahim   Please – no violence.

Dina   If you don't leave, I'm going to start screaming for help.

Goonda   If you scream, we'll have to stop you.

Dina   Stop him, please! Do something.

The **Goonda** *spits on the cloth, spraying it with paan juice.* **Maneck** *tries to attack him.*

Maneck   You bastard.

Goonda *stops him.*

Goonda   Okay. You've had your fun, bacha.

He brandishes a knife. **Dina** *screams.*

Ibrahim   Put that away. Orders didn't say anything about beatings and knives.

Goonda   We haven't come here to kill cockroach with our shoe.

Ibrahim (*to* **Goonda**)   Your work is done. Ja.

Goonda   We should set fire to the place.

Ibrahim   And burn whole building? Then what would landlord say? Now go. I am in charge.

Goonda *goes off menacingly.*

Ibrahim   I'm sorry, sister . . . I'm sorry, sister.

Ishvar   You have no shame! Trying to destroy this poor lady. What kind of monster are you?

Ibrahim   Just doing my job . . . I didn't know he would . . .

Dina   You didn't know? You brought him?

Ibrahim *breaks down.*

Ibrahim   It's no use . . . I cannot do this job. Forgive me, sister. When I brought him, I didn't know he would do such damage. I follow landlord's orders. He tells me to threaten, I threaten; he tells me to plead, I plead. If he raves that a tenant has to be evicted, I repeat the raving at the tenant's door. Like a parrot. You think I am evil? Like everyone else. But I am not . . . believe me . . . it's this job.

Where is justice, sister? I ask the maker of the universe every day, but I expect nothing from him. I am sorry, sister. They will return in forty-eight hours. Your furniture and belongings will be on the pavement. I'm sorry, sister. I'm sorry, sister . . .

Dina I won't open the door to them.

Ibrahim They will bring police to break lock. In this Emergency, they can buy necessary police order.

Dina Who am I harming with my work?

Ibrahim You know, your work is just an excuse, sister. These old flats worth fortune. But not with sitting tenant.

Dina You tell that landlord of yours, Dina Dalal is not leaving. Over my dead body will I ever give up this flat.

Interval.

Act Two

Scene One

Dina's *flat. Some time has passed.* **Dina**, **Maneck** *and the tailors are working. The doorbell rings.* **Dina** *goes to answer it. It is* **Beggarmaster**.

Beggarmaster Namaste.

Dina Namaste. Please sit. When you didn't come on Thursday as usual I was afraid . . .

Beggarmaster That you had lost your protector?

Ishvar You are usually so punctual, Beggarmaster.

Beggarmaster Sorry, I was delayed by an emergency.

Dina This wretched Emergency creating trouble for everyone.

Beggarmaster No, that Emergency has been a boon to me. When fear is on the increase, so is my turnover. No, no . . . I was delayed by a small business emergency . . . I just got the message that two of my beggars, a husband and wife team, who had disappeared mysteriously a while ago . . . well, it seems they were murdered and their bodies have just been found. Police wanted me to make disposal arrangements.

Maneck What evil person would kill poor beggars?

Beggarmaster Happens all the time. They are killed for their beggings. But this case is very peculiar. Money was not touched. Must be some kind of maniac. Only their hair was taken.

Om *and* **Ishvar** *look at each other, the truth dawning on them.*

Dina You mean the hair from their head?

Beggarmaster Han. Cropped right off. They had long luscious hair. They used to spend hours cleaning it for each other; nit-picking, combing it, washing it every time it rained or a water pipe burst on their pavement. I used to tell them, 'It's not good for business, mess it up, make it look pathetic.' Now their tresses have cost them their life and I will have to recruit two more beggars. Know anyone?

Dina, *shocked, shakes her head.*

Beggarmaster   Well, if you see someone who qualifies, let me know.

Maneck   What are the requirements?

Beggarmaster   There has to be a unique feature in the candidates. Let me show you.

He takes out a sketch from his briefcase.

I call it 'the spirit of collaboration'. The blind man will carry the cripple on his shoulders. A living, breathing image of the ancient story of friendship and co-operation. Is it not a thing of beauty? The hitch is to find a blind beggar strong enough or a lame beggar light enough.

Maneck   Wouldn't Shankar be suitable?

Beggarmaster   No. I wouldn't want him to fall off.

Om   But with practice?

Beggarmaster   No!

Ishvar *notices that* **Om** *has said the wrong thing.*

Ishvar   Anyway, he's growing fatter on the jalebis you treat him with daily.

Beggarmaster   I don't treat him enough. If only I could keep him in comfort and happiness for ever.

Om   But he's very happy.

Beggarmaster   Because he knows no different. My friends, let me share something with you. A few weeks after I saved you and Shankar from that irrigation project, one of my beggarwomen who was dying wanted to confess something to me. She told me she was Shankar's mother. No great surprise. I always remember her as a young girl, suckling a baby. Nosey we called her, because of her disfigured face. Beautiful body she had, though. That baby was Shankar. He was separated from her and sent for professional modifications by my father who was Beggarmaster before me. He circulated Shankar among all his female beggars. Drunken bastard never told anyone that it was him that had enjoyed Nosey's body and left her pregnant. I only believed her when I verified it for myself. Shankar has an extra bone sticking from the nape of his neck, same as my father. So, you see, Shankar and I are brothers.

Ishvar   Brothers . . .

Beggarmaster   Please keep my confidence and swear not to tell Shankar. I am not sure how he will take it.

Maneck   Surely he would he happy if he knew?

Beggarmaster   What if the story of his early years makes him bitter and unforgiving to my father and me?

Dina   Truth can hurt.

Beggarmaster   Nosey told me she loved my father. The only man who could look upon her face and still adore her.

Dina   Surely that would be a comfort to Shankar?

Beggarmaster   I'm not sure I have the courage to rock his world. What a legacy my stepmother left me. Freaks, that's what we are, all of us. Now I have to arrange for the medical college to pick up the bodies. Just think, my beggars helping in the pursuit of knowledge.

He gets up to go.

Dina *(handing over a brown envelope)*   I had the envelope ready. It includes Om and Ishvar's instalments.

Maneck   I still can't believe how you got the landlord to pay Dina Auntie damages.

Beggarmaster   A contract with me is better that contract with any insurance company.

Dina   I still have nightmares about Ibrahim and his goonda.

Beggarmaster   That goonda has met with an unfortunate accident with his fingers. He can barely give a child a thappur.

Maneck   What happened?

Beggarmaster   That's just detail. Dinabai, as long as you are my clients, you can sleep easy. Work is regular again?

Dina (*hesitant*)   Han.

Beggarmaster   Good, my instalments have to be regular. Acha Namaste.

He goes.

Maneck   What a crazy story. His life is like a *Mahabharat*.

Dina   The only reason I put up with him is because he protects the flat.

Maneck   Who would kill for hair?

Dina   Could only happen in this city.

Ishvar (*getting up to go to the verandah*)   We need to pack, Dinabai, for our journey.

Dina   You notice I didn't tell Beggarmaster you were going away.

Ishvar   You should have. It's not a secret.

Dina   This marriage mania of yours, it will ruin my business.

Ishvar   Dinabai, it is my duty

Dina   It's not as though Om Prakash is longing for a wife.

Om   I tell him he should find himself a wife first.

Ishvar   And you should be quiet before I soften your bones. Ashraf chacha has improved our standing; everyone knows that Om is working for big export company in the city. He has written that there are four families interested in Om.

Maneck   Om is a handsome fellow. Look at his chikna hair style. Top-notch girls will line up by the dozen.

Om   You tell your family to hitch you up. Then your smile will be inverted.

Ishvar   But we can only reserve a girl if we finalise straight away.

Maneck   Like a train ticket.

Om *and* **Maneck** *laugh.*

Ishvar   You shouldn't make fun of things you don't understand.

Om   Maneck is the same age as me. His parents are not hurrying to fix his wedding.

Ishvar   These families are in a hurry. There are other parties with marriageable sons, so we have to decide straight away.

Dina   That's a gun to his head. Say 'No' to them.

Ishvar   Who are you to tell me what is best for my nephew?

Dina   Just giving good advice.

Ishvar   What do you know about us, about his upbringing, about my duty, that you think you can advise on such matters?

Dina   Fine. Don't expect me then to find food and shelter for wife and children when they arrive.

Ishvar   I don't expect anything from you. We work for you, we are not your slaves that you can tell us how to live and when to die. If you wish, we will go back to our village.

Dina   Go. Do what you like.

Maneck   Auntie!

Dina   After all I've done! Taken them into my home, treated them like family. This is how he talks to me.

Ishvar   Om's marriage is my one duty in life. Nothing else matters.

Silence.

Dina   Three of you, on the verandah? Where is the privacy?

Ishvar   You come with me and see how people live? Eight, nine people in a small room. Sleeping on top of each other, like goods in a warehouse.

Dina   You don't have to lecture me, I have lived in this city all my life.

Ishvar   So, compared to such misery, the verandah is de luxe lodging. If he wants privacy, I can go and have a beedi for few hours.

Silence.

Dina   Well, I suppose we can try it out.

Ishvar   You will see, the minute she crosses over your threshold. Daughter-in-laws can transform the destiny of a household.

Dina   She will be neither my daughter-in-law, nor yours.

Om *and* **Ishvar** *go out onto the verandah and take the hair packet out of the trunk.*

Om   You think Rajaram is the killer of those beggars?

Ishvar   My heart says he is.

Om   It's unbelievable. He seemed such a nice person.

Ishvar   What sort of person makes a living by collecting hair?

Om   Maybe it was an accident.

Ishvar   These are desperate times.

Om   You saw how he was looking at Dinabai's hair?

Ishvar   Don't add any more chilli and masala to the story. Maybe we should report to the police.

Om   You might as well complain to that crow in the window.

Ishvar   If he has killed for these, he'll come for them back.

Om   But we are leaving.

Ishvar   We can't pollute Dinabai's home with the evidence of this madman's collection. Go and give this bag to Worm, don't tell Shankar anything. Just tell him to pass the bag on.

Scene Two

Beggarmaster *brings* **Shankar** *to where* **Rajaram** *has set up his pavement barber-stall.*

Beggarmaster   I've got a special treat for you today.

Shankar   Another treat?

Beggarmaster   You tired of treats?

Shankar   It's not my birthday.

Beggarmaster   You can never have too much happiness in life.

Shankar   The other beggars are asking what I have done to deserve your kindness?

Beggarmaster   You tell them to dare to ask me?

Shankar   You taking me to prostitute?

Beggarmaster   Better than prostitute. (*To* **Rajaram**.) Arey, you do massage, shave as well as haircut?

Rajaram   Han, han, for you, Beggarmaster, I've got special de luxe package.

Beggarmaster   Not for me, for my friend here, I want you to give him the works.

Rajaram   You?

Shankar   Kesa hai?

Beggarmaster   You know him?

Rajaram   Who doesn't know this beggar?

Beggarmaster   He might be a beggar to you, but I love him dearly.

Rajaram   If you spruce him up too much, people won't give him money.

Beggarmaster   Fuck them! Now can you do this or not?

Rajaram   Of course. You come back in two hours. I'll give him the pampering of his life.

Beggarmaster *goes.*

Rajaram   So, face maalish first. Or haircut?

Shankar   I don't want haircut.

Rajaram   But you need cut.

Shankar   No, babu. I don't want it. I like long hair.

Rajaram   I'll cut carefully and give you dandruff treatment.

Shankar   No.

He takes the ponytails out of the package.

I want you to fix this to my hair. Permanent.

Rajaram   Where did you get this? But this is my hair? How did you get this?

Shankar   Om and Ishvar gave it to give back to you. But I like it.

Rajaram   You shouldn't be sneaking in the bag.

Shankar   But it feels soft and beautiful.

Rajaram   Give it to me!

Shankar   My Beggarmaster wants you to give me what I want. I want you to glue this to my hair.

Rajaram   You are out of your mind. Give me those back!

Shankar   No, I want soft long hair.

Rajaram   Look, keep your voice down. Give me those. I'll bring some special glue and do it tomorrow.

Shankar   I want my long hair right now!

Rajaram *runs off as* **Shankar** *is left with a crowd calling for his blood.*

Voice   Sala, murderer!

Voice   He must be the murderer!

Voice   Psychopath!

Voice   What a monster! Killing for hair!

Voice   Rot in hell, you monster!

Shankar *flees through the menacing crowd on his platform, onto the busy road – where he is killed.*

Scene Three

Shankar's *funeral procession.*

Beggar 1   He was always smiling – even as a baby with a nipple in his mouth his face lit up.

Beggar 2   He is with God now, free as a bird.

Beggar 3   And we are left with this bastard Emergency.

Beggarmaster   I should have put brakes on his gaadi, but it seemed silly. He was not a rally driver.

Beggar 4   I saw it. He lost control and flew off the pavement, straight into a double-decker bus. Both Shankar and his gaadi crushed completely . . . together.

Beggarmaster   I had to identify him. In all my years in this profession, my eyes have seen much that is gruesome. But nothing like this. The wood and castors embedded in his flesh will have to burn with his mutilated body.

Beggar 1   When he is reborn, he will surely have sturdy legs that run like the God of Wind.

Beggar 3   I'm going to miss his voice – 'Oh babu, ek paisa dedo.'

Beggar 2   One time Beggarmaster treated him to a prostitute – he let me go instead to cheer me up.

Beggar 1   Born beggar but with the heart of a king.

Beggar 4   Beggarmaster, you've spared no expense. Mountains of fresh rose petals to sprinkle on his body.

Beggar 1   Don't think any of us are going to get same lavish treatment.

Beggarmaster   He was my brother and he died not knowing. I waited too long to tell him . . .

The **Beggars** *start singing an evocative Hindi song about friendship:* *'Ye dosti hum nahin bhoolenge.'*

Dina *and* **Maneck** *are to one side.*

Maneck   I have never been to a Hindu funeral. Do you think they'll be a strong smell, Dina Auntie?

Dina   We don't have to go to the cremation. We've shown our faces.

Maneck   I want to, and not just to show my face.

Dina   You should be studying for your exams.

Maneck   I don't want to argue, Auntie. I'm going.

Dina   I can't stop you, but if you go, I go with you.

Maneck   Shankar is getting quite a send-off. So many people who loved him.

Dina   Whereas at our Parsi funerals, people come for gossip and finger-wagging.

Nusswan *comes up to them.*

Nusswan   Dina! What on earth are you doing here?

Dina   Attending a funeral.

Nusswan   Must be someone important. The traffic's at a standstill. I had to abandon my car.

Dina   You'll collapse on the street without your air-conditioning.

Nusswan   So who is this VIP that you know?

Dina   I do know a few important people, you know.

Nusswan   You going to keep me in suspense?

Dina   Shankar, a beggar.

Nusswan   What?

Dina   You're face is going red. You'll explode any second.

Nusswan   You and your warped sense of humour. Who is it really? The MD of Au Revoir?

Maneck   It's true, sir.

Nusswan   Why are you two attending a beggar's funeral?

Maneck   He was a friend.

Nusswan   Now I've heard it all. You're coming with me, both of you.

Dina   I'm paying my condolences.

Nusswan   How low are you going to sink?

Dina   Look, I'm an adult.

Nusswan   Then behave like one. What will people say if they see my sister prancing in a procession of beggars?

Dina   You can tell them I've been brainwashed by the underworld, but you're praying for my soul.

Nusswan   Your tongue is becoming as loose as the low-lifers you mix with.

Dina   You're sweating. Careful, or your BP will shoot up.

Nusswan   As if you would care.

Dina   I do care.

Nusswan   You have a fine way of showing it.

Dina   I'm leading my life. You lead yours.

Nusswan *grabs* **Dina**'s *arm.* **Beggarmaster** *comes up to them.*

Nusswan   Are you coming?

Beggarmaster   Is this man bothering you?

Dina   Not at all. He's my brother. He was offering condolences for Shankar's death.

Beggarmaster   You are all honouring Shankar by being here. May I invite you to join us?

Nusswan   I'm very busy. Sorry. I must go.

He leaves.

Dina   I am sorry I never met Shankar, but Om and Ishwar spoke very highly of him.

Maneck   He was a lovely person. Shankar looked after them on the site.

Beggarmaster   Just as well the tailors are not here. Grief would have ruined the wedding. And marriage is like death, only happens once.

Dina   I wish more people would understand this.

Beggarmaster   Come. Let us send Shankar off on his continuous journey. (*To* **Maneck**.) Don't worry. It's a beautiful sight. A completeness, a calmness, a perfect balance between life and death.

The procession moves and **Dina** *and* **Maneck** *follow.*

Maneck   I wonder how Om's bride-selection is going.

Scene Four

Market day in the small town where **Ashraf** *lives. Various vendors, stalls. etc., selling their wares. Film songs interrupted by various messages of the nation's need for birth control, rewards in store for those willing to be sterilised, etc.* **Om**, **Ishvar** *and* **Ashraf** *walk through, eating candyfloss.*

Ashraf   I wanted so much to gift you a shirt each.

Ishvar   But Ashraf chacha, we couldn't let you spend good money on those.

Om   The buttons were badly sewn, the pocket was crooked and the stripes didn't meet.

Ashraf   Han, these ready-made shirts have stolen all my custom, but I should have known they won't pass the scrutiny of my apprentices.

Om   Everything we know is from you.

Ashraf   If my eyes weren't so bad, I could have sewn you some shirts myself.

Ishvar   Chacha, you have given us enough, it is us who can never repay you.

Ashraf   You prosper in the city, that is all the repayment I need.

Ishvar   So the girls are lined up for Om to see?

Ashraf   Yes, although some in the families were sceptical about me, a Muslim, being the bride-selection committee.

Ishvar   They should know, we are closer than family.

Ashraf   The elders remembered my ties with your father, thank God.

They hear the **Potency Peddlar** *and become fascinated by him.*

Potency Peddlar   Are you having difficulty in producing children? Is your danda reluctant to rise up? Fear not, there is a cure. Like a soldier to attention it will stand. One, two, three – bhoom! Does it stand, but not straight enough? Is there a bend in the tool? Leaning left like the Marxist-Leninist party? To the right like the Jan Singh fascists? Or wobbling mindlessly in the middle like the Congress Party . . . Fear not, for it can be straightened! Does it refuse to harden, even with rubbing and massage? Try my ointment and it will become as hard as the government's heart! Capable of turning all men into engine drivers! Punctual as the trains in the Emergency! Back and forth you will shunt with piston power every night! Apply once a day and your wife will be proud of you. Apply twice a day and she will have to share you with the whole block!

Ishvar Shall we buy you some?

Om I don't need this rubbish.

Ashraf Inshallah, sons and daughters will appear at the proper time.

There is a loudspeaker announcement about sterilisation.

That Thakur Dharamsi has turned every market day into a sterilisation mela.

The **Thakur***'s men move the* **Potency Peddlar** *along.*

Ishvar Is that villain still alive?

Ashraf He's thriving. The district has put him in charge of family planning.

Om Our people should get together and kill that dog.

Ishvar Don't start talking nonsense, Omprakash.

Ashraf My child, that demon is too powerful. Since the Emergency began, his reach has extended from the village to all the way here. He is big man in the Congress Party. They say he will become minister in the next elections.

Ishvar It's him, he's just walked into the square. Avert your eyes!

Om *walks boldly up to the* **Thakur***.* **Ishvar** *pulls him back and he falters. He spits on the pavement a few feet away.*

Thakur I know who you are.

Ishvar You are mad! Bilkool pagaal! If you want to die, why don't you swallow rat poison! Acting like a hero and thinking like a zero.

Om If you hadn't stopped me I would have spat in his face.

Ishvar Have you come for a wedding or a funeral?

Om   My wedding and the Thakur's funeral.

Ashraf   You should forget your vengeful thoughts and stay out of his way.

Ishvar   We're only here for a short time and we'll return to our jobs in the city.

The loud revving of truck engines is heard.

Ashraf   Market has hours to go, why have the garbage trucks arrived?

Ishvar   And a police guard for the bazaar!

Ashraf   Something is wrong.

Potency Peddlar   Sterilisation police!

People run in every direction to escape the police trucks. **Ashraf** *falls and is helped off.*

Scene Five

A woman hums a song to her sleeping baby. **Om** *and* **Ishvar** *join the queue.*

Man   Same old songs they are playing and they haven't offered us any tea yet.

Woman   Arey, be alert. Or they'll give you tubectomy instead of vasectomy.

Ishvar   You are very knowledgeable.

Woman   The radio is drumming it into us.

Om *and* **Ishvar** *move.*

Middle-Aged Man   I told them do it to me, I have fathered three children but my son here is only sixteen! Never married! I hope they spare him.

Ishvar   You see. We can talk to the doctor. Tell him you have no children yet. They'll let you go. Although they are wasting the operation on me. I am never going to marry.

Middle-Aged Man   The more they do, the more that Thakur lines his pockets.

Ishvar   I thought they will pay us.

Middle-Aged Man   You are a simpleton!

Woman   Will you hold my child for me when my turn comes?

Ishvar   Haanji, you don't worry, sister.

Woman   I'm not worried, I'm looking forward to it. I already have five children but my husband won't let me stop. This way he has no choice. Government will put a stop to it.

She sings to her baby.

Na, na, na . . . Narayan,
My sleepy little Narayan.

Ishvar (*to* **Om**)   Narayan. That was your father's name. If you ever have a son, you keep his name alive.

The **Nurse** *comes and ushers* **Ishvar** *and* **Om** *into the tent with the* **Doctor**.

Nurse   You over there, and you next two here . . . collect your things.

Scene Six

Operating tent. The **Doctor** *strides on with the* **Nurse** *at his side.*

Doctor   Thakur Dharamsi is coming later to check the totals. If he is not pleased, we may as well send in our resignations.

Om *and* **Ishvar** *come before the* **Doctor**.

Ishvar   There is a mistake, Doctor-ji. We don't live here. Doctor-ji, you are like mother-father to us poor people. Your good work keeps us healthy. Also I think nussbandhi is very important for the country. I am never going to marry, please do the operation on me. I will be grateful, but please leave out my nephew. Doctor-ji, his name is Om Prakash and his wedding is happening soon, please listen to me, Doctor-ji, I beg of you!

They are pushed around and their pants are removed. **Ishvar** *starts to cry.*

Nurse   He's under.

Ishvar   Please, Doctor-ji, not my nephew! His marriage is being arranged!

Om *says nothing. The* **Ishvar**'s *pleas fall on deaf ears.*

Scene Seven

The **Middle-Aged Man, Om** *and* **Ishvar** *are lying in the recovery area.*

Ishvar *(crying)*   Everything is ruined. Nobody will accept you now for their daughter.

Om   I don't care.

Ishvar   You are a stupid boy. You don't understand what it means! I have let down your dead father! Our family name will die without children, it is the end of everything. Everything is lost!

Om   Maybe for you. But I still have my dignity. I'm not crying like a baby.

Middle-Aged Man   I've heard the operation is reversible.

Ishvar   After the nuss is cut?

Middle-Aged Man   Specialists in big city. They can reconnect the tube.

Ishvar   Are you sure?

Middle-Aged Man   Absolutely sure. Only thing, it's very expensive.

Ishvar   You hear that, Om? There is still hope. Never mind how expensive, we will get it done. We'll sew like crazy for Dinabai, night and day. God bless you. See, my child, we will go back, reverse this nussbundhi and come next year for your wedding. They will be other families interested by them and maybe this accursed Emergency will be over and sanity will return.

Thakur Dharamsi *arrives.*

Middle-Aged Man   It's the Thakur.

Ishvar   Quick, Om, turn your face and cover it with your arms. Pretend that you're asleep.

The **Thakur** *stops at the foot of* **Om***'s mattress and stares. He whispers to the* **Doctor***, who turns pale, and leaves. The* **Doctor** *and* **Nurse** *make* **Om** *stand up.*

Doctor   I need to check you out again.

Ishvar   Why? You already finished his operation. Now what more do they want?

Scene Eight

Doctor   Get him on the table.

He picks up a scalpel.

Testicular tumour. Thakur Dharamsi has authorised removal, as a special favour to the boy.

Om*'s pants taken off. The* **Nurse** *grips a rag of chloroform to his nose. He goes limp.*

Nurse   He's under.

The **Doctor** *removes his testicles.*

Doctor   Don't send this patient home with the others. He will need to sleep here tonight.

Scene Nine

Ishvar   What have you done to him? He went out standing and you bring him back senseless!

Nurse   He was very sick and the doctor did a free operation to save his life. You should be grateful instead of crying.

Ishvar *checks* **Om**. *He notices blood on his trouser crotch. He undoes* **Om**'s *trousers and sees the dressing.*

Nurse   The boy was very sick. His testicles were full of poison. They needed to be removed.

Ishvar   Hai Ram! Look what they have done to my nephew. They have made a eunuch out of him!

Ishvar *weeps. No one can comfort him.*

Scene Ten

A road.

Ishvar, *stumbling with* **Om** *in his arms, comes across a man with a handcart, who stops.*

Man   What is wrong with the boy?

Ishvar   The Thakur's savages have robbed him of his seed.

Man   Hai Ram, the dark age. Kaliyug has surely come.

Ishvar   Not happy with wiping out our entire family, he has made sure the bloodline is finished.

The **Man** *makes a pillow out of his turban and they put* **Om** *on the handcart and push it.* **Om** *screams intermittently.*

Man   Where do you need to get to?

Ishvar   Muzaffar Tailoring, on the main road.

Man   They have also been victim to tragedy.

Ishvar   What?

Man   The old man Ashraf passed away. Accident, they say, from stumbling and hitting head on the kerb.

Ishvar   Hai Ram! He was hit by policeman's lathi yesterday.

Man   Lies become truth in these goondas' wrong hands.

Ishvar   Thank you for telling us. I will go to the funeral.

Man   He was buried straight away.

Ishvar   How life can change in a day!

Scene Eleven

Dina's flat.

Dina is sitting sewing her quilt as **Maneck** comes in with some items to pack in his suitcase.

Maneck   Are you going to spread it on your bed when it's done?

Dina   It's going to be Om's wedding present. A curtain to partition the verandah.

Maneck   Your daughter-in-law will love her bridal suite, Auntie.

Dina   Don't be cheeky.

The bell rings. It is **Beggarmaster**, carrying a kettle.

Dina   Namaste, Beggarmaster. Please come.

Beggarmaster   Are the tailors not back yet?

Dina   I'm hoping next week. Mrs Gupta is also getting impatient.

Beggarmaster   Well, I had bought Om this aluminium tea kettle. Wedding present. I'll bring it again next Thursday.

Dina   There won't be a problem with the landlord, will there? Because the tailors haven't paid.

Beggarmaster   No, no. I am looking after the flat. Don't worry. With such good people, I am not concerned about temporary arrears. You came to Shankar's funeral, I won't forget that.

Dina   Thank you.

Beggarmaster   Sometimes I think I am ready for salvation myself, but for the sake of my wordly duties I must keep my spiritual urges in check.

He gets up to go.

Dina   Beggarmaster, before you go. There was this fellow asking for you. Said he was Monkeyman, but he didn't have any monkeys.

Maneck   He said he had important business with you.

Beggarmaster   He has been after me to give his niece back. As if I take people against their will. She ran to me, snotty-nosed and crying. He was mistreating her, not feeding her so she would remain small and be hoisted up the pole for the entertainment of others. I saw her potential and now she is one of my dependents.

Maneck   Will you give her back?

Beggarmaster   Once my beggars are yoked to me, they can have no other ties.

Dina   Well, I told him you're in this neighbourhood every Thursday.

Beggarmaster   Then he can find me. Namaste.

Dina   Namaste.

Beggarmaster *goes.*

Dina (*about* **Beggarmaster**) He's being reasonable about the money, but for how long?

Maneck   Auntie, I told Mummy to send a cheque for three months' rent. I'm sorry we couldn't give you proper notice.

Dina   Well, jobs in Dubai have to be snapped up straight away.

Maneck   Even this job I only got because of Daddy's contact.

Dina   Does it matter how you got it?

Maneck   It matters to him that he had to go cap in hand to the Brigadier. He arranges my life, but still makes out that I'm abandoning him and his general store.

Dina   Make a success of your job. Your father will be proud.

Maneck   Brigadier Grewal jokes that every Arab has an AC unit to cool their tents in the desert, and with sandstorms choking the motor and fan there's a constant demand for new ones. So I'll be able to make a small fortune. Maybe I can come back in a few years and start my own air-conditioning business or, even better, we could start a tailoring business. I would be the boss, of course.

Dina   You're welcome – especially with your personal skills with village tailors.

Maneck   Will you rent out my room again?

Dina   I have no choice.

Maneck   Anyone who sees your technicolour curtain and tribe of tailors on the verandah will run a mile.

Dina   You better hurry or you'll miss your train.

She goes up to **Maneck** *to say goodbye. He impulsively hugs her and she tentatively responds.*

Dina   Bless you.

Maneck   Goodbye, Auntie.

Dina   I need a refresher course in solitude.

Maneck   Om and Ishwar will be back soon.

Dina   Of course.

Maneck   Will you say goodbye to them from me?

Scene Twelve

Some time passes. **Om** *and* **Ishvar** *are setting off for the station.* **Om** *is pulling* **Ishvar** *on a rolling platform. His legs have been amputated.*

Ishvar   Why are we going back to the city? My life is over. Just throw me in the river by our village.

Om   Don't talk bakwaas yaar.

Ishvar   It's your foolishness that has brought this on us.

Om   For my foolishness, I lost my balls. But how is your sterilisation my fault? And the poison in your legs? Did I do that? We should have stayed in the city, on Dinabai's verandah.

Ishvar   So we should have stayed hidden on the verandah for the rest of our days? What kind of life, what kind of country is this, where we cannot come and go as we please? Is it a sin to visit my native place? To get my nephew married?

Om   Come on. Don't start a drama in the station, yah.

Ishvar   The pain . . . pain in my legs . . . Massage my legs, Om.

Then the realisation hits him that his legs are no longer there.

Sala, why do I still feel them?

Om   At least you still have both hands. You can sew. Dinabai has an old hand machine. She will let you use it when we go back.

Ishvar   You're a crazy boy. I can't sit, I can't move and you are talking of sewing.

Om   And you are giving up.

Ishvar   The first time we took a train to the city, I was full of hopes and dreams for your future. Now I barely have reason to live.

Om   Live because you're alive.

Scene Thirteen

Dina's *flat. A few days have passed.*

Dina *is sewing her quilt when there is a knock on the door.*

Dina (*shouting out*)   If you're from the HP people, take the machines!

Ibrahim   It's me. Ibrahim . . . Please, sister, let me in. Sister, I beg you. It's important. The landlord has dismissed me but I have to warn you, please, sister.

Dina   I don't understand, why would the landlord dismiss you?

Ibrahim   He said I was destructive with office property, that I was breaking too many folders. But the real reason is I have lost my passion for my duties. I am unable to menace the tenants the way I used to. After what happened here with that goonda, I had a realisation, thank God. I am useless to the landlord.

Dina   Have you found other work?

Ibrahim   At my age? Who will hire me? But never mind that. I have come to warn you, you are in great danger from the landlord.

Dina   I am no longer scared of that rascal. Beggarmaster is looking after me.

Ibrahim   But sister, your beggarmaster is dead.

Dina   What? What are you saying? Have you gone crazy?

Ibrahim   No, he was murdered yesterday. I saw it all – I am the police star witness. It was horrible, horrible.

Dina   So who killed Beggarmaster?

Ibrahim   A very sick-looking man. He was hiding behind the stone pillar at the gate. When Beggarmaster entered, he jumped on his back and tried to stab him with a blunt knife. Such a feeble man, anyone could have escaped.

Dina   So why didn't Beggarmaster?

Ibrahim   The weight of the bag of coins chained to his wrist kept him trapped. He fought back with his free arm and kicked about like a demented spider, but finally he stopped moving. He, who lived off the beggings from helpless cripples, died because of them.

Dina   So the killer was after his money?

Ibrahim   No, he just threw down his knife and said he was Monkeyman and he had killed Beggarmaster for revenge.

Dina *is shocked.*

Ibrahim   Are you alright, sister?

Dina   Monkeyman came here last week, asking to meet Beggarmaster for some business. It was me who told him Beggarmaster comes every Thursday . . . yesterday.

Ibrahim   Don't blame yourself, sister. Police said he was a mental case – he didn't even try to run. He was shouting all kinds of nonsense – that Beggarmaster had stolen his niece Chunni, cut off her hands and turned her into a beggar, and now he had his vengeance as was prophesied. Sister, the landlord is getting eviction order against you.

Dina *goes and gets some money out of her handbag and tries to give it to* **Ibrahim**.

Dina   Here –

Ibrahim   You have enough troubles. I can't accept this.

Dina   Then why call me your sister? Here, take it. Just until you find a job.

He takes it.

Ibrahim   You have to act fast, sister.

Dina   What can I do? Run to my brother, run to the court house? File a case when I have no money or hope of winning?

Ibrahim   What happened to your tailors and paying guest?

Dina   Not even the courtesy of a postcard to say 'Please, excuse us, Dinabai, we have decided to settle in the village.' You open up your home and hearth and still people use you and discard you. They've all abandoned me. Tell your landlord to take his wretched flat. It's just bricks and mortar, nothing of the heart and soul that I've put into it.

Scene Fourteen

Ruby *and* **Dina** *are in* **Nusswan**'s *flat.*

Ruby   You are comfortable, Dina? Anything you need, please say. We want you to be happy here. It's your house, no?

Dina   I'm fine. Thank you, Ruby.

Ruby   We'll put your father's cupboard in here. It's been waiting for you. I said to Nusswan, 'Why keep such old things?' But he was very firm. Little sister wanted that old almirah. Your flat was too small, but we kept it for you.

Dina   I don't have enough things to fill it with.

Ruby   Still, looking at it will remind you of old times.

Dina   Yes.

Ruby   The boys will be thrilled to have you back. They really miss their Dina Auntie. Remember, when they were little and you had all the time in the world to play with them. Sometimes I was jealous. They loved their auntie more than their mummy.

Dina   That's not true.

Ruby   Just think, now Nusswan is looking to arrange their marriages. How time flies. You know Zarir has a girlfriend? He thinks I don't know, but you can't fool a mother no? Sorry. You don't have regrets, no? About not having children?

Dina   No.

Ruby   The pleasure and the pain. Anyway, just as well. How would you have managed with children in tow? It's so good to have you back. We can do things together.

Dina   Please, you mustn't change your routine for me.

Ruby   No, no. It's no problem. You were always such a help. I was going to give up my Willingdon Club membership. The fees going to waste, but now maybe I can use it. You don't like to leave the house to servants.

Nusswan *enters.*

Nusswan   Sorry I'm late, darling. These never-ending meetings. Truck brought everything safely?

Dina   Yes, thank you.

Nusswan   If only you'd contacted me before. We could have done something through the courts, but once they'd broken the locks and entered . . . Possession is two-thirds of the law . . .

Dina   Nine-tenths.

Nusswan   Huh?

Ruby   It's nine-tenths of the law.

Nusswan   Yes . . . Yes . . . Your table outside looks like it's from Adam and Eve's time. I'll call a rag-and-bone man to dispose of it.

Dina *doesn't react.*

Nusswan   You didn't bring your Singers?

Ruby (*quietly*)   The HP people took them away.

Nusswan   I suppose your beggars and tailors and paying guest have all wished you *au revoir.*

He laughs at his own joke.

Ruby   Stop it, Nusswan. Be nice to Dina, she's been through a lot.

Nusswan   I'm only teasing. I can't tell you how happy I am that Dina is back. For years and years I have prayed to God to bring you home. It hurt me so much, you choosing to live alone. In the end only family will help, when the rest of the world turns its back on you. No more humiliation with tailors or beggars. No need for them. You don't have to worry about money any more. Just make yourself useful in the house, that's all I ask.

Ruby   Nusswan! Poor Dina always used to help me. One thing she is not is lazy.

Nusswan   I know. I know. Stubborn is what she is, not lazy.

Ruby   I've always admired your strength and determination.

Nusswan   Dina is one in a million. I'll never forget how bravely you behaved when poor Rustom passed away on your third anniversary.

Ruby   Nusswan!

Nusswan   Sorry! Sorry! I'm starving. These people stroll into meetings whenever they feel like. You know the Emergency has lost its novelty. The initial fear that disciplined people, made them punctual and hardworking. That fear only is gone. Government should do something. Give a boost to the programme.

He leaves the room. **Dina** *picks up her quilt and lays it down.*

Ruby   That is beautiful. Absolutely gorgeous! But what happened in that corner – why the gap?

Dina   I ran out of cloth.

Ruby   What a pity. You know, I have some lovely material; it will provide the perfect finishing touches. You can complete it with that.

Dina   Thank you.

Nusswan (*off*)   Darling! I said I was hungry na?

Ruby   Coming!

She goes off, leaving **Dina** *sitting alone.*

The sound of riots is heard, to signify the assassination of Mrs Gandhi. The huge portrait of Mrs Gandhi is slowly lowered. **Dina** *exits and then comes back in a change of costume. Time has passed.*

Scene Fifteen

1984. **Nusswan***'s flat.* **Dina** *is sweeping the floor. The doorbell rings.*

Dina   Well, if it isn't Mac Kohlah.

Maneck   Maneck.

Dina   Come in. You've changed. I hardly recognised you.

Maneck   I went to your flat and you were not there.

Dina   After eight years you appear suddenly out of nowhere.

Maneck   I was in the Gulf.

Dina   I know. What was it like?

Maneck   It was . . . empty.

Dina   Empty?

Maneck   Like a desert.

Dina   Well, it is a desert country. You didn't write to me from there.

Maneck   I didn't write to anyone. Seemed pointless.

Dina   In any case, my address changed.

Maneck   So what happened to the flat?

Dina   What can I say? Life has come full circle, so here I am.

Maneck   Does Nusswan treat you all right?

Dina   You don't have to whisper. Nusswan's at the office and Ruby's at her club.

Maneck   You have enough to eat?

Dina   There is more food here than I have appetite for.

Maneck   What about Ishvar and Om? Where are they working now?

Dina   They are not working.

Maneck   But how are they managing? Especially with Om's wife and children.

Dina   There is no wife, no children. They have become beggars.

Maneck   But that's impossible! Aren't they ashamed to beg? Couldn't they do some other work if there is no tailoring?

Dina   Without knowing anything, you are so quick to judge them.

Maneck   Please, Auntie. Tell me what happened.

Dina   You remember when they went back to arrange Om's wedding? Well, their enemy Thakur Dharamsi spotted them and used his power to crush them.

Maneck   What did he do?

Dina   Om was castrated and Ishvar lost his legs after his sterilisation led to infection.

Maneck   I don't believe it!

Dina   Really? You've forgotten the Emergency and the draconian measures taken by our PM?

Maneck   And now she's been assassinated.

Dina   So what brought you back?

Maneck   My father passed away.

Dina   I am sorry.

Maneck   The store is now mine to do with as I please.

Dina   What will you do with it?

Maneck   Sell it to one of the giant corporates that have invaded the mountains.

Dina   But you loved that store.

Maneck   All I ever wanted was to stay in the mountains and run the shop, but he wouldn't even let me rearrange the shelves.

Dina   If you hadn't left, we all would never have met.

Maneck   That's true, Auntie.

Dina   Look, Om and Ishwar will be here in half an hour. They come every day at one o'clock. If you're not in a hurry you can meet them.

Maneck   I'm sorry. I can't stay. I have so much to do before I leave for the mountains tomorrow.

Dina   I am sorry. Maybe you'll come again. Meet Om and Ish next time.

Maneck   Yes. Next time. Bye-bye, Dina Auntie.

Dina   Bye, Maneck.

Scene Sixteen

Maneck *passes* **Om** *and* **Ishvar** *on his platform in the street.*
Ishvar *is on the quilt, which is faded and frayed. He jingles his tin.*

Ishvar   Arey babu. Ek paisa dede?

Maneck *pretends not to recognise* **Om** *and* **Ishvar**. *He walks on.*

Scene Seventeen

Nusswan's *flat.*

Soft knock. **Dina** *ushers the tailors in. She gives them water and food.*

Dina   Anyone saw you come in?

Ishvar   Nahin, Dinabai.

Dina   Eat quickly. My sister-in-law is coming home earlier than usual.

Om   Chappatis are a little dry.

Dina   They are from last night, Nawab sahib. I had a visitor. You'll never guess who?

Om   Mac. We saw him passing. He didn't recognise us.

Ishvar   I even said, 'Oh babu ek paisa dedo', to get his attention.

Dina   I asked him to wait and meet you but he said 'next time'.

Ishvar   That will be nice.

Om   The Maneck we knew would have waited today.

Dina   When you go far away, you change. Distance is a difficult thing. Remember, tomorrow is Saturday, everyone will be home. You mustn't come for two days.

Ishvar *moves a thread from the quilt which is tangled around the castors.*

Ishvar   Oh hoi, what's this?

Om   Let me see. A thread has got unravelled.

Dina   Good thing you saw it, or that piece might have fallen off completely.

Ishvar   It's easy to fix. Can I borrow your needle, Dinabai? For a few minutes?

Dina   Not today. I told you. Ruby is returning early.

She gives him a needle and a spool.

Take this with you.

They go outside. She realises they've forgotten the green pagoda umbrella that Rustom gave her. She goes inside, gets it and follows them out.

Dina   You forgot your umbrella.

Ishvar   It was very useful last night. I hit a thief who tried to grab our coins.

He raises the rope and hauls it, imitating a bullock driver, with **Om** *being the bullock.*

Dina   Stop it. If you behave like that on the pavement, no one will give you a single paisa.

Ishvar   Come on, Pyare! Lift your hoofs or I'll give you a dose of opium!

Dina *laughs as they emerge onto the street.* **Ishvar** *calls out for coins.*

Ishvar   Eh babu, ek paisa dedo!

Glossary of Hindi Words

Aaja	Come here
Aapne	Ours (as in 'our people')
Acha	Yes
Adab	Urdu greeting
Almirah	Cupboard
Arey	A cry used to get someone's attention or as an exclamation. Rather like 'Hey!'
Baal	Hair
Babu	Literally, clerk
Babul ki duaen leti jaa	'Take your father's blessing's with you.' Here quoted from a famous Hindi song often sung at weddings when a daughter is leaving her father's house to live with her in-laws
Bachu	Child, often used in a derogatory way when putting someone down
Badmash	Rascal or villain
Bakwaas	Rubbish
Beedi	Cheap, roll-up cigarettes
Behna	Sister
Beta	Little one
Bhajia	Fritters made from chick-pea flour and vegetables
Bhenchod	Sister-fucker
Bilkool pagaal!	Totally mad!
Bus karo	That's enough
Chacha	Uncle; literally, 'father's younger brother'
Chai leke aa	Bring some tea
Chikna	Literally, 'sticky', but in 'chikna hairstyle', as here, a trendy hairstyle using lots of oil
Chini jyada dalna	Put more sugar
Choli	Sari blouse
Chotu	Little one
Chup kur!	Be quiet!
Dall	Lentils
Danda	Stick
Dekho	Look

Eh Babu ek paisa de do

	Spare a paisa, sir
Gaddi	Literally, 'car', but in this case referring to the little makeshift platform with wheels that Shankar the beggar rides around on
Goonda	Thug
Hai	It is
Hai Bhagwan!	Oh God!
Hai Ram	Oh Lord Ram (as in 'Oh God!')
Han	Yes
Hena?	Isn't it?
Idhar aa	Come here
Inshallah	God willing
Kachra	Rubbish
Kaliyug	The dark age
Kesa hai?	How are you?

Khana table pe lag gaya he

	Food is on the table
Khutt khutt	Chit chat or bickering
Kismet	Fate
Koi	Someone or anyone
Kum	Less

Kya hua jo dil tuta

	'What happened that my heart has broken?' In this case, the words of a famous Hindi film song
Kya kahen?	What can I say?
Kya mutlub?	What do you mean?
Kyon?	Why?
Lathi	Heavy stick, often used for beating
Lord Hanuman	The monkey god who saves Sita from the demon king Raavan
Maalish	Massage
Maderchod	Motherfucker
Masala	A mixture of spices. To add masala to the story is to embellish it like food with more spices
Maya	Illusion; often used to talk about the world being nothing but illusion

Mela	Fair
Moksha	Salvation, to be freed from the endless cycle of rebirth
Muzdur	Labourer
Nahin	No
Namaste	Hindu greeting
Nehari	Delicacy made of beef or lamb, which takes hours to cook
Nuss	Tube
Nussbundhi	Vasectomy
Oh Hero ke bache!	O son of a hero!
Paan	Betel nut wrapped in a leaf and eaten as a digestive
Pahle chachi ko salaam kar	
	First greet your auntie
Paisa	The smallest coin; a hundred paisas make up a rupee
Pani	Water
Piche hato!	Get back
Prasad	Sweets offered after prayer or to the gods
Pyare!	Beloved!
Raen de	Leave it
Raja ki aayegi baraat	
	'The King will come as a groom with his procession.' Here the words of a famous Hindi film song
Roti	Chappati
Sala	Literally, 'brother-in-law', used as an expletive
Salaam	Greeting
Shabash	Well done
So Ja	Go to sleep
Socha he?	Have you thought?
Suer ka bacha!	Son of a pig!
Tamasha	A spectacle
Thakur	Landowner
Thappur	Slap
To kese chalta he?	So how goes it?
Toh	So
Yaar	Friend

Ye dosti hum nahin chodhenge
　　　　　　'I will never leave this friendship.' Here the
　　　　　　words from a famous Hindi film song
Yeh to nahin ho sakta
　　　　　　This can't be done

Methuen Drama Student Editions

Methuen Drama Modern Plays

include work by

Edward Albee
Jean Anouilh
John Arden
Margaretta D'Arcy
Peter Barnes
Sebastian Barry
Brendan Behan
Dermot Bolger
Edward Bond
Bertolt Brecht
Howard Brenton
Anthony Burgess
Simon Burke
Jim Cartwright
Caryl Churchill
Noël Coward
Lucinda Coxon
Sarah Daniels
Nick Darke
Nick Dear
Shelagh Delaney
David Edgar
David Eldridge
Dario Fo
Michael Frayn
John Godber
Paul Godfrey
David Greig
John Guare
Peter Handke
David Harrower
Jonathan Harvey
Iain Heggie
Declan Hughes
Terry Johnson
Sarah Kane
Charlotte Keatley
Barrie Keeffe
Howard Korder

Robert Lepage
Doug Lucie
Martin McDonagh
John McGrath
Terrence McNally
David Mamet
Patrick Marber
Arthur Miller
Mtwa, Ngema & Simon
Tom Murphy
Phyllis Nagy
Peter Nichols
Sean O'Brien
Joseph O'Connor
Joe Orton
Louise Page
Joe Penhall
Luigi Pirandello
Stephen Poliakoff
Franca Rame
Mark Ravenhill
Philip Ridley
Reginald Rose
Willy Russell
Jean-Paul Sartre
Sam Shepard
Wole Soyinka
Simon Stephens
Shelagh Stephenson
Peter Straughan
C. P. Taylor
Theatre de Complicite
Theatre Workshop
Sue Townsend
Judy Upton
Timberlake Wertenbaker
Roy Williams
Snoo Wilson
Victoria Wood

Methuen Drama Contemporary Dramatists

include

John Arden (two volumes)
Arden & D'Arcy
Peter Barnes (three volumes)
Sebastian Barry
Dermot Bolger
Edward Bond (eight volumes)
Howard Brenton
   (two volumes)
Richard Cameron
Jim Cartwright
Caryl Churchill
   (two volumes)
Sarah Daniels (two volumes)
Nick Darke
David Edgar (three volumes)
David Eldridge
Ben Elton
Dario Fo (two volumes)
Michael Frayn (three volumes)
John Godber (three volumes)
Paul Godfrey
David Greig
John Guare
Lee Hall (two volumes)
Peter Handke
Jonathan Harvey
   (two volumes)
Declan Hughes
Terry Johnson (three volumes)
Sarah Kane
Barrie Keeffe
Bernard-Marie Koltès
   (two volumes)
David Lan
Bryony Lavery
Deborah Levy
Doug Lucie

David Mamet (four volumes)
Martin McDonagh
Duncan McLean
Anthony Minghella
   (two volumes)
Tom Murphy (five volumes)
Phyllis Nagy
Anthony Neilson
Philip Osment
Gary Owen
Louise Page
Stewart Parker (two volumes)
Joe Penhall
Stephen Poliakoff
   (three volumes)
David Rabe
Mark Ravenhill
Christina Reid
Philip Ridley
Willy Russell
Eric-Emmanuel Schmitt
Ntozake Shange
Sam Shepard (two volumes)
Wole Soyinka (two volumes)
Simon Stephens
Shelagh Stephenson
David Storey (three volumes)
Sue Townsend
Judy Upton
Michel Vinaver
   (two volumes)
Arnold Wesker (two volumes)
Michael Wilcox
Roy Williams (two volumes)
Snoo Wilson (two volumes)
David Wood (two volumes)
Victoria Wood

For a complete catalogue
of Methuen Drama titles
write to:

Methuen Drama
A & C Black Publishers Limited
38 Soho Square
London W1D 3HB

or you can visit our website at
www.acblack.com